Take Five

Best Contemporary Tanka

Volume 2

Take Five

Best Contemporary Tanka

Volume 2

2009

Edited by
M. Kei, editor-in-chief (USA)
Sanford Goldstein (Japan)
Patricia Prime (New Zealand)
Kala Ramesh (India)
Alexis Rotella (USA)
Angela Leuck (Canada)

MODERN ENGLISH TANKA PRESS
BALTIMORE, MARYLAND
2010

THE UNEXAMINED LIFE IS NOT WORTH LIVING.
SOCRATES

MODERN ENGLISH TANKA PRESS
Post Office Box 43717
Baltimore, Maryland 21236 USA
www.themetpress.com
publisher@themetpress.com

Take Five: Best Contemporary Tanka, Volume 2

Copyright © 2010 by M. Kei.

Front cover art, "September Sky" (acrylic) Copyright © 2001 by Alexis Rotella. Used by permission.

All rights reserved. No part of this book may be reproduced in any form or by any electronic or mechanical means including information storage and retrieval systems without permission in writing from the publisher, except by a scholar or reviewer who may quote brief passages. See our Educational Use Notice at the end of the book.

Take Five: Best Contemporary Tanka
Edited by M. Kei, Sanford Goldstein, Patricia Prime, Kala Ramesh, Alexis Rotella, and Angela Leuck.

Printed in the United States of America. 2010.

ISBN 978-1-935398-20-2

publisher@themetpress.com
www.themetpress.com

Acknowledgments

The editors wish to thank the many editors, poets, and fans who submitted books, journals, websites, photocopies, PDFs, and other materials for our perusal. This year we reviewed over 140 venues and sixteen thousand poems. Without their support it would have been impossible.
Additional thanks are due to Collin Barber for his assistance during the early part of the project.

Table of Contents

Introduction, 9
Individual Tanka, 25
Tanka Prose, 155
Tanka Sequences, 163
Editor Biographies, 173
Credits, 179
List of Venues, 189

Introduction:
Tanka in the Electronic Age

<u>Part I</u>
Take Five : Best Contemporary Tanka is now an annual rite. The extraordinary labor and lofty goal of the first volume invited skepticism; the results won high praise and broad appeal. Volume Two required even more labor and broadens the field still further; this year's editorial team read sixteen thousand poems and over a hundred and forty venues. The expansion was due largely to a convergence of poets, editors, and small presses coming together through the opportunities provided by electronic publishing and social media. Volume One, necessarily foundational, surveyed the history of tanka in Japanese and English. Volume Two looks forward, tracing out exciting new developments and the increasingly democratic appeal of the form.

The single most important venue for tanka publication today is Twitter. This social media site, limited to posts of no more than one hundred and forty characters, had already become home to #micropoetry of several sorts, including #haiku and #senryu. ('Hashtags' starting with # are used to simplify following and searches. Following #tanka will deliver all recent tweets with the keyword #tanka in them.) Various excellent tanka poets publishing on Twitter, such as Kris Lindbeck, Sean Greenlaw, David Lee Kirkland, Dirk Johnson, Marin Paul, Kathy Nyugen, Carole Johnston, Alex von Vaupel, Aki Gibbons, and more, had never or only rarely been published in the print media. (Some of them are published in this anthology.)

Twitter poets engage in a variety of online games, networking, and publications; they enjoy the ability to retweet (repost) items they liked, sharing them with their friends and followers, and getting almost instant responses from their readers. Poets want to be read, and Twitter provides one of the most facile mediums yet invented to connect poets and readers. Very few of these poets have attempted to participate in the established tanka world. Why bother submitting to the 'gatekeeping' process of traditional journals when anything can be published on Twitter with a minimum of technical skills and an immediate audience? Gone are the days of waiting weeks, months, and sometimes years between submission and publication. They are not ignorant of conventional tanka forums—quite the contrary: they enjoy reading them. They just don't see the point of submitting to them.

Formally edited microjournals such as *7x20* exist on Twitter; while other editors cull the tweets for worthy works which they archive and share (with the permission of the original posters), such as the *Dragonfly Archive*. A number of tweeters informally edit personal archives by deliberating following and retweeting #micropoetry such as #tanka. Several pirate microjournals have come and gone, while several new legitimate microjournals, such as *microcosms*, are anticipated to begin publication in 2010—and some of them are even paying poets for their work! Various mainstream poetry journals have devoted issues to Twitter poetry, and various bloggers have compiled lists of Twitter poets and poetry. The #micropoetry community accepted tanka as soon as they became aware of it; it was one of the quickest and warmest welcomes tanka has received.

As tanka poets from the traditional publishing world like M. Kei, Alexis Rotella, Denis M. Garrison, Mike Rehling, Carol Raisfeld, Marty Baird, Jeanne Emrich,

Paul Smith, Chen-ou Liu, Naia, and Magdalena Dale, discovered Twitter, they also discovered the possibilities of poetic connectivity. Many established poets share poems that had originally appeared in the print media, but many also offer original poems of high quality that have never been published anywhere but Twitter.

Editors will also tweet samples of poetry to advertise and promote a particular journal or book. Given that a poet on Twitter may have hundreds of followers, an individual poet's readership is easily as large as most of the print journals. When popular poems are retweeted by multiple followers who also have followers who retweet, a tanka may reach a readership of several thousand in a matter of hours. If it gets picked up by a major tweeter who may have tens of thousands of followers, the audience swiftly dwarfs the conventional tanka readership. Even if only a few of those readers become fans of tanka, the readership enlarges and diversifies.

Each person who retweets a tanka passes judgment on it: "This is good, I want to share this." It is the most democratic form of editing yet invented. Above and beyond that, readers can ask questions and engage tanka poets in discussions. Due to the succinct nature of tweets, the didactic posts are tanka-esque in themselves. Nonetheless, a surprisingly amount of information can be conveyed in a hundred and forty characters. Informal discussions illuminate various points about tanka for readers and poets alike.

The editorial team at *Take Five* reviewed more than two thousand tanka on Twitter alone. Twitter thus rivals *Modern English Tanka* in the sheer mass of tanka published on an annual basis. The overall quality is just as good and varied. Given the collected readership of the various poets, Twitter's audience is as large as MET's, but more ephemeral. Most tweets have a lifespan of only a few weeks before disappearing under the flood tide of continuing tweets. Thus the development of archival journals, such as the *Dragonfly Archive*, that cull poetry from the tweet stream to republish on websites in a conscious effort to preserve this highly transient form of literature.

Along with Twitter, several other electronic media have become home to tanka poets. The most notable is Scribd.com. Poets can post entire documents, random poems, articles, and ebooks to be sold or downloaded or read for free on the site. Several journals are experimenting with archiving copies on Scribd.com. Many tanka poets have chosen to reprint electronic versions of older books via Scribd. Given that the goal of the *Take Five* editorial team is to read all tanka in a given year, reprints—including electronic reprints—are eligible for consideration. As long as the reprint was published in the year under consideration, and the original had not been previously reviewed by a *Take Five* team, it was eligible for consideration. Thus, when all twelve issues of *Modern English Tanka* were published on Scribd.com, the reprinted issues 1-6, which were published in 2006-2007 before *Take Five* was established, were eligible, but issues 7-12 were reviewed by the 2008 and 2009 teams in their first editions. The reader will find a number of fine tanka from *Modern English Tanka* here.

In addition to the major electronic venues, a variety of other venues have sprung up to deliver tanka by toolbar and other devices. A number of poetry workshop sites have added tanka to their forums, and some have hosted tanka contests. Some of them are home to distinctively voiced urban communities that utilize street language and reflect the concerns of African Americans, working class people, youth, and other communities not well-represented in the mainstream of tanka publication. These developing poets were viewed with interest by the *Take Five* team. Several of them show promise, and hopefully with more seasoning will rise to the level suitable for publication in *Take Five*. The development of such alternative voices is a welcome diversification of tanka in English and proves that tanka is a suitable vehicle for poets of any background. That tanka has already made the leap from classical Japanese to modern English is proof of its flexibility, durability, and suitability for any approach or subject matter.

2009 saw continuing publications in the field of hybrid print and electronic media pioneered by MET Press. Numerous journals in the MET Press stable operated on both levels; the print journals provided a modest amount of funding to support the larger online audiences. However, at the end of 2009, Denis M. Garrison, publisher of MET Press, announced that he had to reduce his workload for personal reasons. Several MET Press journals closed or were spun off to other publishers. *Atlas Poetica* moved to Keibooks, and *Prune Juice* transferred editorship and publication responsibilities to Liam Wilkinson. Both journals continue publishing, but *Modern English Tanka* closed and has not been revived at this time. Its digital editions remain online. MET Press simultaneously curtailed its equity publishing arrangements. MET Press was a major driver of tanka publication from its founding in 2006; above and beyond its own sizable catalog of publications, it demonstrated a new model utilizing print-on-demand (POD) technology that enabled more poets, editors, and journals to achieve affordable quality print publication. Several small presses formerly active in the print world are making the move to POD publishing, such as Winfred Press and AHA Books.

2009's contraction saw the demise of *American Tanka*. Although a revival effort was announced, it did not publish any issues in 2009. Likewise, Jane

Reichhold, founder and editor of the *Tanka Splendor Award* for twenty years, announced the closing of that contest. *Simply Haiku* also announced its permanent closing. Efforts are under way to revive *Simply Haiku*, but it is too early know if they will be successful. *Brevities* is incommunicado and appears to have ceased publication. *Rusty Tea Kettle* published one issue and went dormant. *Wisteria* is on hiatus. Most recently, Jeffrey Woodward announced the end of *Modern Haibun & Tanka Prose*.

All is not grim in the Tankatown; *Magnapoets* expanded by offering two fine small anthologies and *Eucalypt* continues offering its Tanka Challenges. Several long standing short poem journals such as *Lilliput Review* and *bottle rockets* continue publishing on a consistent basis. Mohammed Siqquidi continues to edit, publish, and give away at his own expense the *Seasons Greetings Newsletter,* which is an anthology of classic and modern tanka and haiku. *Atlas Poetica* has expanded to thrice a year publication beginning in 2010. Other venues have changed form: *3Lights Gallery* has become the *3Lights Journal*. Workhorses of the genre, such as *Ribbons, The International Tanka Contest* by the Tanka Society of America, and the *San Francisco International Tanka Contest* by the Haiku Poets of Northern California continue. New journals have joined the ranks, such as *Notes from the Gean* which publishes short poetry in an online journal. The *Lyrical Passion* website has added a Tanka Corner and sponsored a Tanka Contest. *Moonbathing*, a journal for women tanka poets, was announced and published its first issue early in 2010.

Although publishers do not share their web statistics, the online versions of *Modern English Tanka, Simply Haiku,* and *Atlas Poetica* were rumored to have monthly readerships in excess of five thousand unique visitors. As more poets, editors, and publishers become aware of the reach of digital media, the conversation has begun to shift from 'publication' to 'audience'. Partly this reflects the performance nature of tanka (it originated as an oral art), but it also reflects the changing concept of tanka poet from 'writer' to something else. Exactly what that 'something else' is remains to be seen.

Certainly we are seeing more storytelling in tanka; the genre of tanka prose continues to develop and is outstripping the tanka sequence in popularity. Even so, long narrative sequences are being published which present a 'slice of life' or 'shasei' as the Japanese call it. Utilizing an online publication means that sequences too long or to expensive to be published by traditional means can now be published. The apparent dearth of tanka sequences may be an artifact of previously existing journals being unable or unwilling to include it. It's hard to justify devoting ten pages of a fifty page journal to a lengthy tanka sequence. After the demise of *Modern English Tanka,* only *Atlas Poetica* is left as a journal that expressly includes tanka sequences (including very long sequences) as part of its publishing mission.

In addition, more tanka poets are establishing blogs and personal websites. These media often have a narrative quality in which the poet shares commentary, stories, and framing information in connection with the poetry. Some incorporate music and visual arts in their presentations. Poets report sharing their poetry in public gardens, at dinner parties, and during multi-art presentations incorporating music, poetry, food, visual arts, dance, and other elements. In short, tanka is returning to its ancient Japanese origin as a communal activity embedded in the lives of the people.

The editorial team for *Take Five* attempts to read all tanka published in a given year. 2009 marks a transitional point at which it becomes increasingly difficult to define 'published' and to accommodate the burgeoning variety of ways in which tanka is shared with its audience. Still, the bulk of the work published in 2009 is presented in a fixed textual form, even if it is the score of a musical piece. Take Five does not evaluate the non-literary aspects of the tanka; it is impossible to present music, art, dance, scenery, food, and other non-textual aspects of a poetry presentation. This means illustrated tanka and musical tanka can be evaluated by the team solely for their literary merit; that is to say, their merit as they appear in text. That, and the sheer size of the body of tanka literature, means that many fine poems cannot be included due to limitations of space and technology. Readers are encouraged to view the anthology as a travel guide: a map to discover literary worlds worthy of further exploration.

<u>Part II</u>
This year's poetry is highly diverse and spans the English-language history of tanka. We are pleased to publish several poems by Kisaburo Konoshima (1893 - 1984), with English translations by David Callner. Konoshima represents one of the old school Japanese tanka poets of the mid-20th century. His grandson, David Callner, rightly recognized his grandfather's poetry as being significant in the history of tanka in North America, so he translated and published a bilingual edition of *Hudson, a collection of tanka*, in 2004, making it one of the few books of North American tanka to be republished. Since then he has been publishing some of his grandfather's other tanka in *Simply Haiku : A Quarterly Journal of Japanese Short Poetry*. Several of them appear in this anthology.

眠れぬままに夜半を起き出ほろ苦き日本茶いれて老をたのしむ

> Unable to sleep I rise in the dead of night
> pour some slightly bitter Japanese tea and enjoy being old

無意識に所かまはず放屁する悪癖さへも我れ亡父に似て

> Breaking wind anywhere I like
> I take after father even in bad habits.

These two tanka give an idea of the range of Konoshima's work. The former would be at home in any of the mainstream tanka journals, while the latter has an earthy humor rarely seen in what can be a highly mannered genre.

At the opposite end of the spectrum of time and culture is a young poet, Sean Greenlaw. Rarely published in traditional print venues, he posts his tanka on Twitter. Young enough to be the son or grandson of most of the poets published in the anthology, his skill can stand beside the best known poets in the genre.

> twenty three dollars
> in the bank account
> these days
> even a crow's cackle
> will shake my bones

Very few poets can be both ruthless and sensitive at the same time; in Greenlaw's work beauty and reality meld to form a merciless truth. Very often tanka poets are tempted into nostalgia, sentimentality, or spirituality to redeem difficult subjects and make them palatable. Comfortable poetry is popular and enjoyable, but it does not shake the bones. Greenlaw's work most closely resembles Sanford Goldstein's, although culturally and spiritually they are continents apart.

Goldstein has been writing tanka of extraordinary honesty for more than four decades. At eighty-four he is the oldest tanka poet still writing and publishing today, and has had the longest tanka career of any living tanka poet working in English:

another
Father's day
I did
not visit
his grave

Co-translator of modern classics of Japanese tanka, Goldstein knows the Japanese tradition and has adapted it with seemingly effortless ease to English. His Father's Day poem is one that says everything it needs in thirteen syllables.

Stylistically James Tipton is at the other end of the tanka spectrum. His full-bodied tanka have a richly conversational tone, replete with observations of life as it is lived in the flesh. Even so, what is left unsaid is just as important as what is written:

That *señorita* who just boarded
can take all the time
in the world
to stuff her obstinate luggage
into the bin above me.

Probably most men would not mind the *señorita* and her luggage, either. A more thoughtful perusal might cause us to wonder who the *señorita* is, where she is going, and why. We might ask the same about the narrator as well. Now that they have encountered each other, what happens? Do they go their separate ways, or become fellow travelers? Such thoughts will no doubt

Best Contemporary Tanka

prompt the reader to perambulate through their own memories of travels and fleeting encounters.

Every editor in *Take Five* was struck by very different poems from the anthology. Patricia Prime chose to reflect on a tanka by Beverley George:

slicing a lemon
with my sharpest knife
seeds remain in place
segments hold their structure
despite my child's divorce

"The imagery in this scene—the interior where the poet slices a lemon—places the domestic world at an almost surreal remove from the trauma which has taken place in the family. For this moment, from within the safety of the kitchen, everything appears peaceful. The remoteness of this inner world of domesticity from the heart-rending fact of a child's divorce is also a symptom of one's powerlessness in the face of the break up of a marriage. The acidity of the lemon, the sharpness of the knife, become a metaphor for the break up of the relationship. But even while the trauma is being relived by the poet, she is able to say 'seeds remain in place / segments hold their structure.' I take this to indicate that though a relationship has ended and while there will be inevitable changes in the future, the family will remain steadfast and supportive.

"The rhythm of the tanka is melodious despite its subject matter. The poem is full of alliteration and assonance. The sibilance of 's' sounds bind the poem and the two 'd's in the last line add an air of finality to the tanka."~Patricia Prime

Human experience has long been the staple of the tanka genre whether written by the courtiers of ancient Japan or contemporary poets. Editor Sanford Goldstein chose a poem by Robert Kusch to comment on:

singing
I've been workin' on the railroad
to the wall
the one happy man
in the Alzheimer ward

"So many poems I admire in Best of 2009. I chose a poet I know nothing about, for his poem on the human condition and the contradictions of that condition grabbed me." ~Sanford Goldstein.

Some poets begin by writing a haiku and tacking on a couple of extra lines to create a tanka, but Kusch's poem makes it clear that the last two lines of a tanka are not 'extra' at all: they are the heart of the poem. Good tanka can work transformations within the space of five short lines.

Angela Leuck chose a very different view of human nature in a poem by ai li:

evening
between her breasts
sugar to lick off
the cocktail glass
rim

"One of the reasons I was originally drawn to tanka was my fascination with the sensuality and suggestiveness of the ancient waka written primarily by women of the court during the Heian Period (794-1185) in Japan. This tanka by the British poet ai li captures that long ago spirit while being at the same time completely contemporary.

"Each short line of this minimalist tanka conjures up a powerful image. There is a titillating tension between the lines, as we, the reader, are pulled between meanings. The poet also uses the senses to great effect. In the first line we have a feeling of darkness. The visual sense of darkness is heightened in the second line by narrowing the focus to the area of shadow between the woman's breasts. 'Sugar to lick off' engages our sense of taste by reference to sugar which we all know and which now involves us intimately in the scene. The cocktail glass inevitably invites comparison between the shape of the glass and the curve of the woman's breast. The choice of the single word 'rim' in the last line is startling in that we can almost feel the rim beneath our tongues, the danger of glass which can so easily shatter. In just a few choice words the danger and excitement of the moment are palpable."~Angela Leuck

Although serious tanka are well-represented in the anthology, and indeed in the genre as a whole, a number of kyoka appear as well. Very few Japanese kyoka have been translated into English, with Robin Gill's *Mad in Translation* being the most substantial. Kyoka have probably existed as long as tanka, but were rarely written down. Characterized by word play, humor, puns, satire and vernacular language, kyoka were popular during the centuries in which the courtly waka tradition was slowly stagnating. Waka had to be in good taste in keeping with the courtly elegance of the Imperial court that was the principle producer and audience for it. By contrast kyoka could be written in ordinarily language about ordinary subjects, and satires of the 'high brow' literature were frequent.

Editor Alexis Rotella, as well known for her senyru as her tanka, has embraced kyoka. She has chosen the following poem by Sanford Goldstein:

> after
> the back-row
> question,
> the pencil in the prof's mouth
> breaks

"This kyoka, upon first reading, gave me a jolt, a shock and a laugh, all at the same time. I thought of the saying, 'Out of the mouth of babes . . .' One can see so clearly the yellow pencil (yellow alluding to things related to the mind) being broken by a comment from a student in the back row. The student may not be the one who always speaks up in class, but one who is often quiet, mostly a listener, but who one day opens his mouth and like a crack of thunder out of the blue, the professor like an old brittle tree is struck open by a bolt of truth. In fact, one wonders if Goldstein was not himself such a student or if he were the professor writing about a student he will never forget."~Alexis Rotella

The poem startles the reader by presenting a very real moment—haven't we all been in a class where a student asked an inappropriate question, resulting in startled laughter and a general break down of classroom order? Such vivid yet human moments give a new vitality to tanka by breaking down the overly refined approach that inherently creeps into a genre that is keenly aware of its courtly past. In the Meiji period (late 19th century) under the influence of reformers like Shiki and the Tekkans, the term 'tanka' was adopted to signify modernization of the form. Modern tanka admit all subject matter and all approaches; as a result there is no longer a need for kyoka so it has all but disappeared in Japan. In recent years tanka in English, which has long paid homage to the classical poets of the Heian period, has become more aware of the many different strands of tanka development in Japan, including kyoka.

While the human experience is the stuff of which tanka are made, some of the most breathtaking tanka in the anthology are not about humanity, but something much larger. They reach the sublime through the ordinary. The shasei, or 'sketch from life', was an approach pioneered by Shiki (1867 - 1902). He was influenced by Western artists and his tanka using this technique resemble the quick sketches of Western artists. Strongly imagistic, shasei tanka have the virtue of good photographs: they capture a moment yet say so much more than what is present on the page. Consider this tanka by Kala Ramesh:

in the curve
of her hip
she holds
an earthen pot's
tilted twilight

On the surface the poem is simple enough: A woman is holding a clay pot. It could be any woman; but the curved hip, the curved pot, and the dark mouth of the pot suggest that this is Woman-As-Goddess, She who will bring something new into the world from her dark and fecund center.

The combination of prose and tanka grants a lucent vision as Adelaide B. Shaw visits '42 Daggett Street.' Past and present dovetail and transform the poet. The change defies words, but it is there in the poet's silent return to her automobile. It is like Schrodinger's Cat: not until the box is opened can the observer know whether the cat is alive or dead. The poet has looked, and so, by the strange alchemy of looking, both she and the neighborhood have changed.

Although the human experience is the usual focus of tanka, Larry Kimmel requires us to move past the merely human to experience the anguish of a snake hit by a car. Usually roadkill causes us the avert our eyes and give it no further thought; but Kimmel's depiction of the snake's death throes (we must hope it died, and quickly, too) forces us to confront the suffering of one of God's mute creatures and to acknowledge our own role in its destruction.

In Angela Leuck's 'Day of the Irises,' the flowers evoke soldiers going off to war and mad Ophelia who drowned herself for the sake of lost love. Love and tragedy mingle inextricably with the flowers, and in the end we will all be unspoken love poems, blinking in the dusk like fireflies. Tanka and the ephemeral tragedies and triumphs of the human world are nothing more than the blink of a firefly's light—but with one difference. We are literate. We can write them down. The courtiers of fourteen hundred years ago are dust, but their poems, like fireflies, have not gone extinct. If we dream for a moment that our own poems will live as long, it is because we are mortal and fear death.

~K~

M. Kei
editor-in-chief, Take Five : Contemporary Tanka

Individual Tanka

A. A. Marcoff

a woman guides
the blind man—
translates
the river light
into words

A. Thiagarajan

for each om
an inhale and an exhale
counting the holds
with an ear on the doorbell
for the morning milk

Take Five, Volume Two

ai li

evening
between her breasts
sugar to lick off
the cocktail glass
rim

Alex von Vaupel

you want to talk
but i have nothing
to say
around our silence
rain falls

autumn . . . watching the leaves and everything else
fall apart . . . all over again

Alexis Rotella

After we fed each other fondue
and inhaled each other's smoke
I said I'd slip
into something comfortable
and chose the back door.

Smoked salmon
on his breath—
our marmalade cat
has been visiting
the Germans again.

Family home for sale—
his brother grabs
the silver,
my husband
his grandpa's poems.

By the third *sanctus*
my mind wanders
out to the parking lot
where he waits
in a white convertible.

Slowly she descends
into the darkness
of the underworld
my mother's hand
slipping from mine.

You say
   you like
my chestnut hair . . .
   how long before
   we're lovers?

My brother-in-law
who speaks eleven languages
fluently
although he doesn't
speak to us.

After dark—
are the male
Greek statues
in the museum
ravishing one another?

Amelia Fielden

look how tenderly
the child is lifted
from her wheel-chair
by this father who longed
for Little League sons

a dark brick house
shrouded in lace curtains
secrets and lies
what a sad price to pay
for respectability

next-door neighbor
as uptight as his tulips
budded gold
in the box hanging off
his immaculate window

I'm reading
rereading his letters
the answer
to my question lies
in what is not there

is this now
what my life has become
plodding along
admiring the seascape
kept company by dogs

in the food court
he mounts an argument
for divorce—
she nods mechanically
spoon-feeding their infant

An Xiao

i know all about
feminism and women's
liberation, yes—
but i have a seat now
and you, sir, do not

Ana-Maria DiVera

my son's eyes
becoming browner
as he drinks
a slow cup
of Mexican hot chocolate

an'ya

I make a mental note
on the eve of my estranged
brother's birthday . . .
what is the big dipper
without the little one

september second
landlocked more than fifty years
and missing the sea . . .
that certain smell of salt wind
only an albatross knows

returning monarchs
. . . I wish I were a tree
this time of year
to feel their velvet wings
embracing my branches

André Surridge

flicker of light
like a white butterfly
in the corner
of one eye—
start of a migraine

I'd like to fly
if everyone else did
said the twelve year old
otherwise it would be
kind of conspicuous

I catch your wave
in the rear vision mirror—
in hindsight
the day was better
than expected

can't play
but still I pine for my guitar
stolen
by a gypsy girl
forty years ago

Andrew Cook-Jolicoeur

this rainy night,
cherry blossoms long gone,
under these trees
I wish for shelter
in a man's arms

Andrew Riutta

ashamed
to look into the eyes
of that beautiful stripper
I drove home,
stopping for a pizza on the way

Angela Leuck

looking up
from a Russian novel
I suddenly notice
the sadness in the faces
of people passing by

young anarchists—
after the second bottle
of vodka
the poster of Trotsky
slips from the wall

Yom Kippur
from sundown
to sundown
we think of nothing
but food

peonies
in bloom
he leaves me
a poem
on the kitchen table

he photographs
fires all day
my neighbour
with the smouldering
eyes

Annette Mineo

so much waiting
in this life
when will they come
the lively red-winged blackbirds
to my lonely marsh again

Audrey Olberg

    tiny tiny buttons
        on the back
        of her blouse
    he's afraid
        she expects too much

Aurora Antonovic

family lines—
I know if I trace
back far enough
I'll find I belong
to someone

after the surgery
he crawled in bed beside me
to cradle me with his warmth—
it was then I understood
the concept of husband

Aya Yuhki

the elderly couple
walk in the middle of
a flurry
of falling cherry blossoms—
some things never end

Barbara Strang

alone
in the old family home—
meeting mine
from a faded photograph
my dead sister's eyes

Becky DeVito

in the warehouse district
remnants of cloth
measured and folded
so many textures
to sadness

Belinda Broughton

plump breasts
in a little black dress
the adolescent girl
so indecisive
about crossing the street

Bell Gale Chevigny

the paper's not ready
the child explained
when it wasn't delivered
because the people
haven't been killed yet

Beverley George

grey-haired now
but when her sister visits
she hides
the wedgwood teapot
that once was their mother's

slicing a lemon
with my sharpest knife
seeds remain in place
segments hold their structure
despite my child's divorce

half a world away
I say your name, light candles,
in all the old cathedrals
their puny flare no contest
for the disease consuming you

five bowls from Japan
lined up on my kitchen shelf
each day
I take one down at random—
this small ritual of choice

gliding about
in wide-legged silk pajamas
Katie Hepburn style
I'm admired . . .
by me, the kids, the cat

where is he going
this bearded, dirty man
clutching a box
of unblemished roses
as if he had the right?

my father
would not allow
caged birds
one day he left us . . .
for the land of long white cloud

New Zealand is known as "The Land of the The Long White Cloud"

Bob Lucky

not a Romantic
of the long-suffering school
I prefer
diseases that come
and go with a cure

mismatched socks
tea stains down my shirt
even lost at solitaire—
if I were a gambling man
today's the day I'd quit

admiring
bikini-clad mannequins
in a shop window
I catch the gray
sneaking into my mustache

at the sushi bar
the drunk drones on about
one that got away
with a wave of his chopsticks
he sends sashimi flying

in a paddy field
outside of Danang
a water buffalo
drags an old plough
into the new year

at a crossroads
in Ho Chi Minh City
I gain insight
into all those chickens
who did not cross the street

in a box
in my mother's attic
a worn journal
in the beam of a flashlight
an old darkness comes to light

C. W. Hawes

the days, months, and years
they've all slipped through my fingers
and what do I have
two teacups on the table
one of which remains empty

C. William Hinderliter

winter solstice
visiting dad
at the graveyard
even now
I find nothing to say

Carol Raisfeld

in the back
of a dresser drawer,
a photograph
when she was very young
who was the man beside her?

Carole MacRury

at the door
in a jacket of red plaid . . .
a blind date
outshines the bouquet
held in his hand

in the squeeze
of your hand when I least
expect it. . .
a stab of loss as if
you were already gone

every room
of this empty house
thick with silence
in this brief separation
a taste of forever

all that's left
of the old homestead . . .
a foundation
filled with flax, larkspur
and prairie grasses

Carolyn Eldridge-Alfonzetti

pumping petrol
this autumn morning
numbers swirl
five? six? or seven days
since we last made love?

stopped
by a magpie's
ochre eye
noticing everything
this first day of spring

Carolyn Thomas

without electricity—
my mother-in-law reads
into the afternoon
by the light
of new snow

Viet Nam—
torn seam of the red kimono
my brother sent me from the war
i wish
he could have met my son

Best Contemporary Tanka

Cathy **Drinkwater** Better

how did you find me
after all these years
coming to visit
when I am no longer
the person you sought

Take Five, Volume Two

Chad Lee Robinson

old blue car—
my father
opens a door
to the boy
he used to be

Chen-ou Liu

my soul
can soar over the Pacific
yet my feet
know the enclosing walls
of an attic room

Cherie Hunter Day

a distant jet
cutting the bluest portion
of the sky in two
my son hasn't called home
in nearly three weeks

Claudia Coutu-Radmore

so difficult
to leave them
so hard to fight
the purple gravity
of lilacs

Colin Stewart Jones

still
trying to catch snow
on my tongue . . .
the bittersweet names
of my aborted child

Collin Barber

noon breeze . . .
a butterfly lands
in the photograph
I would have taken
if I had a camera

another summer —
am I any more alive
than these tulips
dropping their petals
on the kitchen table?

last day of vacation . . .
the notebook I wanted
to fill with poetry
is empty
except for sand

if I let you
out of your cage
canary
can you do
the same for me

Cor van den Heuvel

after the party
I wait alone a long time
in the subway station
dawn over the East River
spreads in all directions

Curtis Dunlap

a recurring dream:
the two of us parked
in your car, laughing,
in the cemetery
where you are buried

Cynthia Rowe

    you gave me
    this conch shell . . . polished
    to perfection
    now you lie on your bed
    no longer hearing the sea

Dave Bacharach

a November sky
filled with geese
headed north—
I've made the same
kind of mistake

I pick one stone
from the creek bed
to take home
it was like any other
until I touched it

I sold my horn
to pay the rent and feed
a child
at night in bed
my fingers play a dirge

her breasts bounce
as she crosses against
a red light
a girl so young
I drag my eyes away

Dave Bachelor

on the same day
place a spray of white blossoms
on my wife's grave
hand a bouquet of red roses
to our only daughter

David Lee Kirkland

Buoyed by the breeze
a red-tailed hawk floats higher
searching for a sign
long after the eulogy
one graveside mourner remains

David Rice

my grandson asleep
in the baby carrier
the weight
of wanting to live longer
heavy on my shoulders

extra extra high
I throw my grandson
the ball
my father rarely
threw to me

David Terelinck

the scent
of freshly mown grass—
you ask
if my long-dead father
will be in for morning tea

Dawn Bruce

after you left
I planted no more bulbs
yet this year
in a neglected corner
a shout of daffodils

Deborah P. Kolodji

"for sale sign"
in front of our old house
I wish I could buy it again
but without you
this time

Denis M. Garrison

this brisk morning walk
more than by my sweater's warmth
I am comforted
by the crisp chill on my cheeks
by the breezes through my beard

fund-raising dinner
slides of starving children
flash quickly by—
the tinkle of crystal
and silver almost stops

the grain bin
where the hired man died
razed to the ground
already the footpath
is filling with weeds

hours before dawn
drinking vodka on the porch
while others sleep
I turn off the light
and give the moth a break

Don Miller

my best friend and I
at our high school reunion
thirty years later
neither one of us where
we thought we would be

Dorothy McLaughlin

just two weeks
after our wedding day
the tux you rented
goes off to dance
with someone else's gown

an overnight bag
for the weeklong visit
how much faith he has
in the long range weather forecast
and our washing machine

Take Five, Volume Two

Elaine Riddell

three years dead
'go easy on the earth'
the message
on his letterbox
still speaks to the world

Ferris Gilli

stuck in the traffic
of a Veteran's Day parade
a one-legged man
swipes my windshield with a rag
until I pay him to stop

Francis Masat

rest home parlor puzzle —
putting in the same piece
I put in last week
I am asked again
what day it is

Gautam Nadkarni

my married friend
who tells me I did right
by remaining single
goes home to a hot meal
and a warm cozy bed

Geert Verbeke

wind has free play
icicles grow quickly
into sharp needles
dad hums a cradle song
from days long gone

George Swede

another friend has slipped
into the long and crowded
history of us—
the fish market's
thousands of open eyes

Minus a few photos
all of mother's albums
went to recycling—
crematorium smoke
rises into rain

The body knows more
than the mind
about many things—
gazed at from behind
the woman looks back

The carnie moves
three shells around
then shows the pea—
this could be
a haiku workshop

H. Gene Murtha

people change
like the color of
a bunting
I feel at peace
when I'm alone

J. Andrew Lockhart

we walk slowly
down the crowded sidewalk
in the rain,
forgetting my age— hoping
you will do the same

summer left
without saying goodbye—
waking up
in the cool morning,
my arms holding a pillow

Jade Pandora

when he's away
I'm a june bug
banging
against a screen
on a summer's night

James Tipton

I used up my whole life
waiting for her to arrive
and now there is nothing left
but her presence here
in a thousand poems.

That *señorita* who just boarded
can take all the time
in the world
to stuff her obstinate luggage
into the bin above me.

I knew she was not for me
which is why I permitted
only part of me
to follow her
into her apartment.

Maybe they're right—
we all have a "soul mate."
Walking through this Mexican village
I know I saw mine today
at least a hundred times.

Jane Reichhold

willows weave
the river on its way
to the sea
following such a path
was how I met my mother

a wave dashes
stone against stone
a click
and a life is gone
into a new grain of sand

a skull of roses
the coming and going
of ants
filled with the ruins
of something loved

Janet Lynn Davis

nonstop footage
of surge-battered homes
  near our back door
  a small displaced turtle
  retreats into its shell

Hurricane Ike, Texas, September, 2008

months later
he still clutches
the bowling ball—
all he could salvage
after Katrina

I fill my head
with a private symphony—
the doctors
discussing my insides
as if I weren't right there

Jean LeBlanc

another semester—
the small high window
of this basement office
with its unrelenting view
of permanent dusk

weave me
a blanket of stories
long into the night
your fingers tangled
in my hair

Jeanne Emrich

within me
is a small house
I tend for us—
this at least is something
I can do well

long winter night . . .
my mind wanders back
to a northern stream
that once answered
my every question

Take Five, Volume Two

Jeffrey Woodward

I sit beside
a lamp
and in the warmth
of that company
turn a page

Jo McInerney

I never had
a wedding ring
just a bond
you threaded through me
like wine through water

Joanne Morcom

if I give you
one more chance to break my heart
the least you can do
is stay around long enough
to pick up the pieces

John Martell

at 80
my neighbors planted
green saplings
and assured me death
would not have the final world

before dawn
silver light from a window
glows on wet pavement
in that long green hour
when widowers start the day

my prowling nights
have long since passed—
still,
when the feline moon is high
I feel an old scar or two

blue ice cracks
on gutter and window sill—
she stands at the sink
soaking the ache from her hands,
the image of her mother

John Quinnett

in his e-mail
my old friend tells me
he's dying
stunned
I click on save

Joyce Sandeen Johnson

this house
has a life of its own
stairs that talk
windows that rattle
shadows that come and go

Take Five, Volume Two

June Moreau

the cat might
buff it with its paw
the august moon
so close
to the open window

Kala Ramesh

I secretly felt
the skirt she was wearing
was gaudy . . .
until a butterfly comes along
in stunning orange

in the curve
of her hip
she holds
an earthen pot's
tilted twilight

the red dot
on my forehead
binds me
to a man
who's in his own orbit

Karen Cesar

who can fathom
this floating world?
pulling the traps
the youngest child returns
a lobster to the sea

the feel of you
so deep inside of me
each movement
bringing us closer
to separation

this scar
connecting belly-button
to pubic mound . . .
yes, there was a time
when I was open

night wind
and pelting rain
the hound
curls more snugly
into the hollow of my back

Kathy Kituai

on arrival
beanie over your ears
you are a stranger—
asleep on the floor   a child
I once held against my breast

packing up
her clothes for charity,
he folds
and unfolds a scarf
still scented with her hair

softer than usual
those women who say Hello
what is it they see
your arthritis   my grey hair
or two lovers holding hands?

my son's eyes
as blue as forget-me-nots
smiling
in photographs
years after his death

by late afternoon
she can no longer ignore
dandelions
placed in a plain jar
lit by sunlight on her desk

Take Five, Volume Two

Kathy Lippard Cobb

my life
a list of things
unfinished
the guitar I can't play
the daughter I don't know

wide awake
from a passionate dream
I watch
the young carpenter
swing his hammer down

Kirsty Karkow

green tea
red plums and oranges
on the blue china
even at breakfast time
this man colors my life

dark of night
moonless, starless
in steady rain
she walks a black dog
toward an empty house

Take Five, Volume Two

Kisaburo Konoshima
David Callner, trans.

眠れぬままに夜半を起き出ほろ苦き日本茶いれて老をたのしむ

Unable to sleep I rise in the dead of night
pour some slightly bitter Japanese tea and enjoy being old

路傍に落ちしマンゴ拾ふは旅の人土着の人はふり向きもせず

Tourists pick up the roadside mangoes
that locals do not even notice

無意識に所かまはず放屁する悪癖さへも我れ亡父に似て

Breaking wind anywhere I like
I take after father even in bad habits

Kozue Uzawa

my acupuncturist
inserts countless needles
around my head,
a small universe full of
worries, regrets, and hopes

Kris Lindbeck

Crochet mags
& Hebrew dictionary
beside me in bed
waking to their smooth covers
I miss your breathing.

Larry Kimmel

we did what we could
read their letters, figured their taxes
good neighbors they—
         now just a cellar hole
and the lilacs in spring

at first light,
before the crack
of dawn—the crack
of an egg
on the skillet's rim

this time, she tells me,
she's telling the truth—
between us
I watch the struggles of a wasp
drowning in peach juice

Laurence Stacey

home
after eight years
in Iraq . . .
my brother now battles
bill collectors

Lenard D. Moore

on the number 4 train
from Brooklyn to Manhattan
I clutch my suitcase—
a young soldier alone
holds his shopping bag

LeRoy Gorman

how lived in
it looks in the dream
a house we never built
with leaves falling
at every window

the drone
of a city going home
fills the hour
you move
from coma to death

Liam Wilkinson

It comes down to this:
the ice-cube and I,
losing our corners
in a glass
of cheap whiskey

under the pier
she kisses me quick,
squeezes me slow —
danger signs
rattle in the wind

bald
all these years
but still stealing
the complimentary
shampoo

a phone call
from an old flame—
constellations
I cannot name
come out of the dark

Coffee, jazz
and a few choice words.
The dawn and I
are getting
brighter and brighter.

Linda Galloway

my daughter
deformed, retarded
prettier
than a tundra blossom
in full bloom

my name,
the third world woman says,
means *white light*
as she changes
my stained hospital sheets

every night
my husband folds his socks
before bed—
how many more socks,
nights are left for us

Linda Jeannette Ward

softly
into the child's room
before darkness settles in
I find the world crayoned
in flames above his bed

bikini-clad
in our small back yard
we soak up rays
and a radio sermon
preached from the neighbor's porch

clearing out
all the things you'd have to
after I'm gone . . .
a strange immortality
in just this moment

last fall's leaves
turning to lullabies
in spring rain
she tells me
of her son's suicide

Lois Harvey

that summer
two brothers paddled
these quiet waters
where today we scatter
one's ashes

Lorelei Jolie Polden

the pointy chin
I never cared for
on myself
so beautiful
  on you

M. Kei

I don't want
to move heaven
and earth,
just the heart
of a man

Melville—
not the great white whale
but your restless heart
I'll take with me and
bury in the sea

Sabbath morning
going down to the sea
and raising the sail,
a white prayer
going up to the sky

cargo shorts,
what dreams
will I stuff
into these pockets
today?

she faded away, my mother,
black hair turning white,
her body fading also,
until all that was left
was the 'O' of her dying mouth

one son dead,
the other shipped
to Afghanistan—
my sister's
long winter

they name
their cats after
stores—
now our neighborhood
has a Macy's and a Sax.

my son does
a load of dishes,
then I do . . .
a pair of bachelors
waking up the moon

M. L. Grace

for thirty years
it wrote on a blackboard
this hand
that now shakes and loses
its grip on soap

my wild side
trapped in an old diary
pages glued shut—
meeting you again
I come completely unstuck

M. L. Harvey

she never made
that promised rag doll
between buttons
in her tin sewing box
the cold stare of eyes

he searches
my hands for signs of work
the cattleman
who sells whole sides of beef
and divines the day by clouds

Magdalena Dale

Frunza uscată
s-a oprit la geamul meu . . .
în van privesc spre
drumul tot mai pustiu
așteptând scrisoarea

A dry leaf
stopped at my window . . .
In vain I look
to the deserted road
waiting for a letter

Margaret Chula

yesterday's desires
what were they?
  a vase
without flowers
holds only itself

walking the path
through the dark garden
  moonlight shines
   on the flower
    with no scent

Margarita M. Engle

trapped
between the pages
of an old book
I brought from Cuba
scent of the sea

feedstore
the scarlet macaw
in a cage
together we dream
of travel

Maria Steyn

war zone—
from the bulletproof vehicle
I glance through the fence
into the pale blue fear
of a soldier's eyes

Marilyn Hazelton

I imagine myself
as a crystal vase
intended for iris
waiting to be filled
by what is yet to be

Marilyn Potter

beside the sea
spray-painted on asphalt
a mandala symbol
fading now
like the hippie in me

Marian Morgan

it should have been
'happy ever after'
but the skin
that your ring encircled
is tanned once more

Mark Rutter

too deep in the cave
for candlelight
to find its shapes—
thunder
of the waterfall

Mary Mageau

our family
unpacks Christmas ornaments
the youngest child
hangs all the stars
on the lowest branch

Max Ryan

work boots
on the sand . . . he sips tea
from his thermos lid,
drifts on the endless blue
of a lunch-hour sea

Megan Arkenberg

late spring
and still no sign
of thaw
you tell me I love you
in all the wrong ways

Melissa Dixon

past midnight—
staring into the dark
again I seek
the sunken doorway
leading down to sleep

awakening
feeling almost invisible
at my age
a sense of expecting
to float away on the tide . . .

Michael Ketchek

in the decanter
by the salad
oil floats on vinegar
I don't shake it again
she's not coming

Michael McClintock

. . . and one day
I acquire everything
needed for my work—
No. 2 lead pencils
and green mountains

starting home, today,
my battered duffle packed
solid as that
mountain over there,
hard against the sky

black-and-white
photographs of family,
not one with a smile;
they are all dead now
and left only these

in a city
drifting among
strangers
sometimes I want
nothing more

enough is enough —
painting the old house
I stop at the eaves
deciding to keep them
cobwebbed and beautiful

I want to join
in that picnic by Renoir
and fix the dangling strap
at the shoulder of the one
whose face is lotion-pink

at the bottom
of a trashcan
a wrapped baby
looking up
at the stars

Miriam Sagan

At the wedding
The guests argued about love
Versus lust
I looked at you in your hat,
Felt both.

In the dream
my dead husband
gives me a hug
his hair has turned gray
in the years he's been dead

It wasn't snow
at all
on the pagoda—
a white silk scarf
tied by the wind

the flowers
on the rich side of town
do what the people
do on the poor side—
burst with color

farmer's market
roast chiles, fiddling,
bunches of carrots—
even here,
each face in a private world

Natalia L. Rudychev

somehow
i feel related
to the tabby
that basks in evening rays
before a night of love

Owen Bullock

I know
you're the woman for me
when I give you flowers
you keep them in a vase
until they're totally dead

quiet evening
I no longer need
the emptiness
to be filled
it can stay as it is

she leaves today
for two months south
on a vineyard
I need to let go a little
of the role of father

Pamela A. Babusci

the knife slips so easily
into the fresh mango
trying to remember
why i hate him
so much

breaking
the red lacquered comb
in two . . .
deep autumn
& still no letter

don't ask
forever of me
i am capable
of loving you to death
one day at a time

alone in spring
she paints her lips
deep fuchsia
the color he hated
the most

bringing a pot of coffee
& cigarettes
to my mother's grave
we have never spoken
so honestly

a van Gogh
starry night
I load
my paint brush with his
torment and despair

one-way ticket
to nowhere
she sits among
the silent
city dwellers

Pamela Cooper

last round of chemo . . .
only one eyelash
remaining
in the clear nighttime sky
a sliver of moon

Pamela Miller Ness

Autumn
of metastasis
she ticks
dozens of exotic lilies
in the bulb catalog.

Patricia Prime

this is the park bench
that waits, always faithful
for my return
where I sit and contemplate
the river's changing moods

without him
she's not too sure.
No one to say
let's have dinner now
or let's have a drink.

I watch
the way an ink line
traverses the page
to become another poem,
unbidden, unwarranted

Patrick M. Pilarski

waking up
your feet
still touching mine
this heavy blanket
of late spring snow

the day
her father died
she clenched her fist
walked to the window
and quietly fed the fish

Paul O. Williams

my wife
in the hospital,
and I reluctant
to go home to the cats,
who all but ask, "Where is she?"

the old couple
walking down the street
displaying
their convincing illusion
of solid permanence

Paul Smith

after your death
I experienced for the first time
as a poet
the inadequacy
of words

watching a moth
hit the window again and again—
that's how it felt
all those years, trying
to get through to you

facing me
on this bright autumn day
two sunflowers—
for once I am happy
to reap what I've sown

Peggy Heinrich

dropping
the sweater I knitted him
into the Goodwill bin . . .
a snow plow
clears the road

Philip Miller

a shadow
in the old snapshot—
all that's left
of the one
who took it

Philomene Kocher

four years on this street
and today I see the fire hydrant
as if for the first time
what else have I walked by
and not really seen

R. K. Singh

At the river
she folds her arms and legs
resting her head
upon the knees and sits
as an island

Randy Brooks

I sit on the edge
of your old couch
afraid to sink in
like one of the family
nodding off to sleep

Raquel D. Bailey

rising from the earth
new hyacinths
to replace the old
a toddler asks
"So when's grandpa coming back?"

robert d. wilson

sundown . . .
an old woman
scooping
fish paste into
recycled bottles

trash piled
up on the side
of the road
like prayers no one
has a need for

may i
slowly undress more
than your clothes?
thoughts of you in
an opera, dancing

i wish i
could pull you out of
a top hat
and make the rest
of the world disappear

buddha stares
past the cries of young
mothers
carrying their babies
through flooded villages

twilight . . .
passersby paint
the walls of
the cemetery
with shadows

a leather doll,
she hobbles up and
down the street,
waiting for the key
in her back to break

Take Five, Volume Two

Reiko Nakagawa
assisted by William I. Elliott

手がしびれからだの中心失ひて杖つく人
を我が身とぞ知る

    My hands are numb,
    my center lost,
    now I know myself
    suddenly
    dependent on a cane.

Robert Kusch

singing
I've been workin' on the railroad
to the wall—
the one happy man
in the Alzheimer's ward

Roberta Beary

all those years
of overtime
for this
an empty house
where children used to live

I fight the urge
to ask them
how to make love last
old couple holding hands
where the waves break

Roger Jones

bang bang bang—
the windblown door
after midnight;
waking from a dream
of a long-dead friend

Ruth Holzer

saffron and black
jacket
of fine Chinese silk—
when will I wear it
in this lonely life?

Sanford Goldstein

like some modern
Aphrodite
risen from turbulent seas,
this Japanese along the beach
combing her long black hair

after
the back-row
question,
the pencil in the prof's mouth
breaks

I look beyond
the coffee shop window
this last day of June
in my childhood I never flew
a kite that high in a swift wind

my corridor pace
to pick up today's junk-mail,
a smile to the clerk
and all the rest—I kick
my shadow in the walk-home sun

I stroke
my mother's grey hair
and she leans
like a withered branch
on my own frail arm

I rise
from my single's bed,
my small bout
with desire
unrequited

faces
at the day-care center
for the aged,
all these foreshadow
the me that is to be

another
Father's day
I did
not visit
his grave

Sean Greenlaw

empty
as the sky
and just as gray
the chipped little bowl
I throw some change into

twenty three dollars
in the bank account
these days
even a crow's cackle
will shake my bones

next to me
filling out an application
for the same job
at a picked through k-mart
a woman twice my age

stanley pelter

she hides her tooth
under a bloodstained pillow
mum much too tired
to act
the wish fairy

Take Five, Volume Two

Susan Marie La Vallee

first star of the night
I make a wish and turn away
feeling quite foolish—
a big girl in big girl shoes
stopping to talk to the sky

Terry Ann Carter

under a yellow parasol
a monk steps off the curb
into sunlight . . .
fire
of a different kind

nothing lives
in the bamboo bird cage
only a memory
of a creature
who sang before dawn

Tess Driver

old spider's web
in a corner of this room—
he took
all our furniture
and the jam jar of small change

Thelma Mariano

winter's end
I wheel her down long hallways
at the home
seeking pools of sunshine
as her own light ebbs away

Tom Clausen

the house quiet
and cold
this early morning alone—
saddened to know how much
I desired just this

the farther away it gets
the more magical it becomes,
those times at night
in the back seat,
my parents taking us someplace . . .

autumn chill
as I go out
to get the paper—
I should just
keep on going

years of thinking
I'll really change
and become a family man
but some little wild weed
keeps growing in me . . .

in the park
someone approaches me,
they have found God
and want to tell me
all about it

all these years
in one house, one job
one town and in me—
too many changes to fathom
as I sweep away autumn leaves

Vasile Moldovan

După plecarea
enoriașilor-biserica goală,
dar pe clopotniță
atâtea ciori disputându-și
cel mai bun loc de pe cruce

    After the flock's
    departure—the empty church,
    but on its spire
    so many chirpy crows claiming
    the best place on a cross

William Hart

the center
of my life
all at once becomes
the gnat drowning
in my eye

Tanka Prose

42 Daggett Street

Adelaide B. Shaw

I lived here for my first 16 years, the upstairs flat in a two family house in an Italian neighborhood. I can still hear my grandfather shouting from the first floor as I went up the back stairs:

"Chiuda la porta."

"Chiuda la luce."

A noisy street and smelly with a Goodyear rubber plant on one corner and a cheese processing plant directly across from our house. Yet a lively and cheerful street with small front gardens and friendly neighbors.

Today, the factories are long closed and empty, along with several of the houses, including ours. The porch roof is gone, the rails sagging. Windows boarded up, concrete where once were hydrangeas, the paint peeling down to bare wood.

Midsummer — the air, in this semi-abandoned neighborhood, is heavy and quiet. I return to the car.

> sudden shouts—
> a man and a woman
> their words unclear;
> on the sidewalk
> shifting litter

On the Verge of Regret

Bob Lucky

on a crowded bus
the beautiful woman's
dark tooth—
my stop is before hers,
which is all I'll ever know

Sitting alone at the kitchen table, which is bare except for a coffee cup and a bottle of Tabasco sauce, I remember Jacaranda trees raining purple blossoms along the streets of Funchal. I get up to look for a bottle of Madeira, but there's not one in the house. In the search, however, the name of a popular bread, bolo do caco, slips off the tip of my tongue, and I wonder if the past ever overwhelms you unexpectedly, if you remember me. You had such a beautiful name, I'm fairly certain, but right now my memory is filled with bread.

foggy morning
mangling the spout
on a milk carton—
life's simple things
require concentration

Reminders

Bob Lucky

over-ripe mangos
on my desk—
reminders
of where I am
where I'd rather be

in the weeks
between heater and AC
a train rumbles through
the night and shakes me
from my sleeping wanderlust

I've never kept a mistress
never killed a man
never climbed Mt. Everest—
at fifty-three
splurging on a rare oolong

My life, on a three-day weekend in Shanghai, is starting to feel like a joke. I'm sitting in an Italian restaurant, nice place with a wood-burning pizza oven, menu by an Italian-Japanese chef from Napoli. A bearded Scotsman in a kilt walks in with an infant in his arms and orders a glass of Champagne. The mother follows with a pram full of shopping bags, orders a salad, and leaves. The salad arrives before she returns. In fact, she doesn't return, and the Scotsman is trying to whisper loudly into his mobile phone and the baby is starting to cry. It can't get any worse. It can't get any better.

In Living Muscle

Larry Kimmel

A taupe snake, thick as a firehose, and like nothing I've ever seen in Massachusetts, before or since, was ejected from beneath the car ahead of mine. It coiled and leapt some three or more feet above the asphalt. There was no time, no way, to miss its writhing hop. It must have leapt at least two times before it was tumbled, with a blunt thumping noise, beneath my own car, and what I saw in the rearview mirror was anguish sculpted in living muscle.

evening breeze,
a quiver travels the driveway's fringe
of ferns
like a shiver of bad news
along a spine

Downsized

Linda Jeannette Ward

> clearing out
> all the things you'd have to
> after I'm gone . . .
> a strange immortality
> in just this moment

Books, bank statements, ten-year-old calendars, more books, photographs never viewed, party clothes never worn—these are the elements of clutter closing in on my life. Emptying drawers, closets and dusty shelves, I wonder how and why I allowed it all to accumulate. It seems my belief in the temporariness of things has been stifled by the pain in my back it takes to move it all out of the way.

How did I fail to notice all along Daddy's living day-to-day epitomized the life I aspired to . . .

> the room
> he inhabited
> I clear after his death:
> two flannel shirts, pants, shoes,
> a carton of cigarettes

The Egyptian Exhibit

Michael McClintock

Names that rattle
like cedar dice in the mouth,
against the teeth:
Akhenaton, Nefertiti,
Tutenkhamen.

Carved in stone three thousand years ago, you are still a child, and the roast duck held an inch from your lips, ready for eating, for all time remains untasted.

I saw your father in the other room, just as you must have seen him, when he stood close, causing your eyes to lift to his and ask no riddles.

Small princess
—naked, breastless—
here you sit
with your ancient dinner,
a sadness for our eyes.

Tanka Sequences

Untitled

Carol Raisfeld

after she died,
sorting through pieces
of mother's life
the shoebox filled with cards
why hadn't I sent nicer ones?

the blue dress
she wore to my wedding . . .
I donate the clothes
that still carry her scent
a strand of hair

in the back
of a dresser drawer,
a photograph
when she was very young
who was the man beside her?

the house bare
on that final night
before leaving
I open all the curtains
to let the stars come in

Day of the Irises

Angela Leuck

from head to toe
in green camouflage
the military man
I glimpsed this morning
on the way to the garden

Mongolian Iris
I wonder
is that soldier
bound
for Afghanistan?

white-tipped
like the Himalayas
King's Spear—
wherever I go
that soldier's on my mind

meadow rue
beside purple irises—
with love
there's always the need
for caution

ghosts of Hamlet
and poor flower-mad
Ophelia—
yellow bearded irises
called *Elsinore*

Moonlight Madonna
bearded iris—
another tribute
to the virgin mother,
the crucified woman

the velvety fur
of the iris's
three outer petals—
who isn't taken in
by softness

it's not so much
the irises
that are beautiful
as the morning light
they're bathed in

the earth is finished
says my science-minded friend
in despair—
take my hand, I tell him,
we'll be fireflies at dusk

iris buds
dipped in blue ink—
I'll paint
an unspoken love poem
on his chest as he sleeps

Legs of Invisible Desire

M. Kei

on the mud
next to the asphalt
a broken doll's head
a crow pecking
at plastic eyes

derelict memory
a broken watch washed up
on a muddy beach
next to the orange foot
of a Canada goose

walking the street
with legs of invisible desire,
looking in windows
at the people for sale
but I have no money

without an audience,
the poet's heart has no meter,
ears give voice
to the red paper
brushing along the ground

nude study

Jean LeBlanc

one hopes he loved her,
the painter, his model,
this little wild thing
caught
in his knowing gaze

one hopes she was warm
while he was busy painting—
her puckered nipples—
no wonder he hurried
the chin

her hand trembled
holding the glass of wine,
as did his—
one hopes for too much
from a canvas, some paint

A Country Visit

Jared Carter

When my grandmother
brought me, many years ago,
we played hide and seek
among the stones. But today,
finding her will not be hard.

First asking his leave,
I clear the weeds from the grave
of my grandfather,
knowing that for many years
he has looked out in this way.

Let us close the gate,
and drive back to the home place.
Up in the old trees
there will still be mourning doves
calling among the shadows.

What is it you fear,
now that autumn is ending?
We two still have time
to bring in the last parsley,
and rake walnuts from the grass.

It is difficult
to contemplate giving up
those two lovely words,
here and now, but I shall not
be needing them much longer.

The sun will still rise
in the east, and the new moon,
and the evening star.
It is only this window
that seems darkened now with mist.

L'Aquila, Italy, 2009

Alexis Rotella

The centenarian
waits for earthquake rescuers
and while she waits
crochets nothing
in particular.

Finally rescued
the old woman
asks
"Can I at least
comb my hair?"

La Bella Figura—
even at
the end of time
we'll be looking
for a mirror.

Editor Biographies

M. Kei

M. Kei is an award-winning poet who lives on the Eastern Shore of the Chesapeake Bay, USA. He is a tall ship sailor who served his apprenticeship aboard a skipjack, a traditional wooden sailboat used to fish for oysters. He is the editor of *Atlas Poetica: A Journal of Poetry of Place in Contemporary Tanka* and the editor-in-chief of the anthology series *Take Five: Best Contemporary Tanka*. His second collection is *Slow Motion: Log of a Chesapeake Bay Skipjack* (2008), a log he kept in verse form while making extended cruises aboard a historic wooden sailing vessel. Over 1200 of his tanka have been published in ten countries and six languages. He also writes non-fiction articles about tanka and compiles the *Bibliography of English-Language Tanka*. He previously edited *Fire Pearls : Short Masterpieces of the Human Heart* (2006) and published a collection of short poetry, *Heron Sea, Short Poems of the Chesapeake Bay*. Most recently he has published a nautical novel, P*irates of the Narrow Seas*, set during the Age of Sail and featuring a gay protagonist.

Sanford Goldstein

Sanford Goldstein, who lives in a village in Japan, continues to write his tanka for more than fifty years.

Patricia Prime

Patricia Prime is the co-editor of the New Zealand haiku journal *Kokako*, assistant editor of Haibun Today, reviews editor of *Takahe* and *Stylus*, and is on the panel of editors for the *Take Five Anthologies, Vol 1* and *2*. She is also one of the judges for the *Presence Seashell Game* and *Metverse Muse* traditional poetry competitions. Her poetry, reviews, interviews and articles have been published worldwide.

Kala Ramesh

Kala Ramesh is an Indian classical musician, having worked extensively on Pandit Kumar Gandharva style under Mrs. Shubhadha Chirmulay for more than 15 years, and has performed professionally in major cities in India. A recently turned haiku poet (since 2005), Kala writes haiku, tanka, senryu, haibun, renku and one-line haiku, and her work has appeared in leading e-zines and anthologies all over the world. Kala heads the World Haiku Club in India. As director, she organised the World Haiku Club Meet at Pune, December 2006. The four-day 9th World Haiku Festival she organized at Bangalore in February 2008 was sponsored jointly by Sri Sri Ravi Shankar Ji and Sri Ratan Tata Trust. She is the Deputy Editor-in-Chief of *The World Haiku Review,* and since April 2009, is also the Poetry Editor of *Katha,* New Delhi, a renowned Indian publishing house. In this capacity, she got together and edited an ebook of haiku, senryu, haibun, tanka and haiga to be published soon, encompassing the work of 35 Indian haiku poets, for the first time in India! Currently, she is also the lead poet (sabiki) of a Kasen renku with six other international renkujin: experimenting and incorporating the traditional renku with the Rasa Theory of India.

Alexis Rotella

Alexis Rotella, founder and first editor of *Prune Juice* (a kyoka journal) is a practitoner of Oriental Medicine in Arnold, Maryland. Read her *Lip Prints* and other tanka books at Scribd.com.

Angela Leuck

Angela Leuck was born in Vancouver in 1960. She obtained a B.A. from the University of Saskatchewan and an M.A. from McGill University. Specializing in Japanese-inspired short poetry forms—haiku, tanka, renga and haibun—she also combines her poetry with collage and photography in an updated version of the Japanese art of haiga. She served two terms as Quebec Regional Coordinator of Haiku Canada and is now Vice President. In 2005, she co-founded Tanka Canada and edited its biannual publication *Gusts: Contemporary Tanka*. She is a full member of the League of Canadian Poets and serves on the board of the Quebec Writers Federation.

An award winning poet, her work has been published in journals and anthologies around the world. She is the author of *haiku white/haiku noir* (carve, 2007), *Flower Heart* (Blue Ginkgo Press, 2006) and has edited a number of anthologies, including *Rose Haiku for Flower Lovers and Gardeners* (Price-Patterson, 2005), *Tulip Haiku* (Shoreline, 2004), and, with Maxianne Berger, *Sun Through the Blinds: Montreal Haiku Today* (Shoreline, 2003). She lives in Montreal.

Credits

Credits abbreviated to save space. Complete citations may be found in the List of Venues Consulted (below). Abbreviations from Tanka Venues approved by the Tanka Society of America <http://TankaCentral.com>

A Thiagarajan
    for each om, EUCL 6
A. A. Marcoff
    a woman guides, BLTH 19:4
Adelaide B. Shaw
    42 Daggett Street, MHTP 2
ai li
    evening, STLT
Alex von Vaupel
    you want to talk, *Tekkan Tanka*.
    autumn, Twitter. http://twitter.com/alexvonvaupel>
Alexis Rotella
    After we fed each other fondue, *rotellagrams*.
    Smoked salmon, *rotellagrams*.
    Family home for sale, *Lip Prints*.
    By the third *sanctus*, Ibid
    slowly she descends, Twitter. <http://twitter.com/mamasanta>
    You say, MH 2009.
    My brother-in-law, *rotellagrams*.
    After dark, *Lip Prints*.
    L'Aquila, Italy, 2009, ATPO 4
Amelia Fielden
    look how tenderly, RIBN 5:3
    a dark brick house, MHTP 2
    next-door neighbor, EUCL 7
    I'm reading, *Tanka Online*
    is this now, SGL.
    in the food court, KOKA 11
An Xiao
    i know all about, STLT
Ana-Maria DiVera
    my son's eyes, RIBN 5:4
an'ya
    I make a mental note, GUST 9
    september second, TTJ 34
    returning monarchs, TTJ 34
André Surridge
    flicker of light, MET 12

I'd like to fly, MET 12
I catch your wave, MET 12
can't play, MET 12
Andrew Cook-Jolicoeur
this rainy night, *My Very Gay Wedding.*
Andrew Riutta
ashamed, RIBN 5:1
Angela Leuck
looking up, RIBN 5:3
young anarchists, SH 7:1
Yom Kippur, SH 7:1
peonies, *A Poet in the Garden.*
he photographs, GUST 9
Day of the Irises, *A Poet in the Garden.*
Annette Mineo
so much waiting, SH 7:1
Audrey Olberg
tiny tiny buttons, GUST 10
Aurora Antonovic
family lines, RIBN 5:1
after the surgery, REDL 5:1
Aya Yuhki
the elderly couple, *Spreading Ripples.*
Barbara Strang
alone, EUCL 6
Becky DeVito
in the warehouse district, GUST 9
Bell Gale Chevigny
the paper's not ready, STLT
Belinda Broughton
plump breasts, RIBN 5:3
Beverley George
grey-haired now, GUST 10
slicing a lemon, [Second Place] *6th Intl Tanka Festival.*
half a world away, PRES 39
five bowls from Japan, TTJ 35
gliding about, RIBN 5:2
my father, MET 12
where is he going, STLT
Bob Lucky
not a Romantic, MET 12
mismatched socks, MET 11
admiring, BLTR 20
at the sushi bar, PRES 37
in a paddy field, *The Year of the Cow/Ox.*
at a crossroads, MET 11
in a box, *Rusty Tea Kettle 1.*

On the Verge of Regret, MHTP 1
Reminders, MHTP 2
C. W. Hawes
the days, months, and years, *Notes From the Gean.*
C. William Hinderliter
winter solstice, PRUJ 2
Carol Raisfeld
in the back, SH 7:2
Untitled, SH 7:2
Carole MacRury
in the squeeze, EUCL 6
at the door, SH 7:2
all that's left, GUST 9
every room, EUCL 7
Carolyn Eldridge-Alfonzetti
pumping petrol, [Certificate of Merit] *6th Intl Tanka Festival.*
stopped, [First Place] *Kokako Tanka Contest.*
Carolyn Thomas
without electricity, REDL 5:2
Viet Nam, REDL 5:2
Cathy Drinkwater Better
how did you find me, RIBN 5:3
Chad Lee Robinson
old blue car, MAGP 4
Chen-ou Liu
my soul, RIBN 5:4
Cherie Hunter Day
a distant jet, RIBN 5:2
Claudia Coutu Radmore
so difficult, *Poet in the Garden.*
Colin Stewart Jones
still, *Rusty Tea Kettle 1.*
Collin Barber
noon breeze, RIBN 5:2
another summer, SH 7:4
last day of vacation, SH 7:4
if I let you, 7:4
Cor van den Heuvel
after the party, REDL 5:1
Curtis Dunlap
a recurring dream, MAGP 4
Cynthia Rowe
you gave me, KOKA 10
Dave Bacharach
a November sky, *While the Light Holds.*
I pick one stone, [Honorable Mention] *The Saigyo Awards.*
I sold my horn, RIBN 5:2

her breasts bounce, SH 7:2
Dave Bachelor
   on the same day, RIBN 5:2
David Lee Kirkland
   Buoyed by the breeze, Twitter. <http://Twitter.com/davidleek>
David Rice
   my grandson asleep, [Third Place] [SFIT]
   extra extra high, MET 12
David Terelinck
   the scent, TTJ 35
Dawn Bruce
   after you left, MAGP 3
Deborah P. Kolodji
   "for sale sign", ATPO 3
Denis M. Garrison
   this brisk morning walk, MAGP 3
   fund-raising dinner, STLT
   the grain bin, *While the Light Holds.*
   hours before dawn, *Rusty Tea Kettle 1.*
Don Miller
   my best friend and I, SH 7:1
Dorothy McLaughlin
   just two weeks, EUCL 7
   an overnight bag [Members Choice] RIBN 5:4
Elaine Riddell
   three years dead, EUCL 6
Ferris Gilli
   stuck in the traffic, STLT
Francis Masat
   rest home parlor puzzle, MET 12
Gautam Nadkarni
   my married friend, RIBN 5:4
Geert Verbeke
   wind has free play, *IJS / ICE.*
George Swede
   another friend has slipped, LILR 168
   Minus a few photos, MAGP 4
   The body knows more, ATPO 3
   The carnie moves, RIBN 5:4
H. Gene Murtha
   people change, *Rusty Tea Kettle 1.*
J. Andrew Lockhart
   we walk slowly, *Past Tense.*
   summer left, Ibid
Jade Pandora
   when he's away, MET 12
James Tipton

I used up my whole life, *All the Horses of Heaven*.
That *señorita* who just boarded, Ibid
I knew she was not for me, Ibid
Maybe they're right, Ibid
Jane Reichhold
willows weave, *A Film of Words*.
a wave dashes, Ibid
a skull of roses, Ibid
Janet Lynn Davis
nonstop footage, MNST 5:1
months later, *Haiku News*.
I fill my head, RIBN 5:2
Jared Carter
A Country Visit, SH 7:2
Jean LeBlanc
another semester, *The Stream Singing Your Name*.
weave me, Ibid
nude study, Ibid
Jeanne Emrich
within me, [Third Prize] *International Tanka Contest*.
long winter night, *Tanka Online*.
Jeffrey Woodward
I sit beside, MET 11
Jo McInerney
I never had, *Notes From the Gean*.
Joanne Morcom
if I give you, GUST 9
John Martell
at 80, EUCL 7
before dawn, EUCL 7
my prowling nights, EUCL 6
blue ice cracks, RIBN 5:4
John Quinnett
in his e-mail, RIBN 5:4
Joyce Sandeen Johnson
this house, RIBN 5:2
June Moreau
the cat might, GUST 9
Kala Ramesh
I secretly felt, STLT
in the curve, MET 12
the red dot, *Rusty Tea Kettle 1*.
Karen Cesar
who can fathom, RIBN 5:2
the feel of you, RIBN 5:3
this scar, *Notes From the Gean*.
night wind, RIBN 5:4

Kathy Kituai
   on arrival, *Straggling Into Winter.*
   packing up, RIBN 5:4
   softer than usual, *Straggling Into Winter.*
   my son's eyes, Ibid
   by late afternoon, Ibid

Kathy Lippard Cobb
   my life, RIBN 5:2
   wide awake, RIBN 5:1

Kirsty Karkow
   green tea, *One Hundred Droplets.*
   dark of night, *Rusty Tea Kettle 1.*

Kisaburo Konoshima, David Callner, trans.
   Unable to sleep, SH 7:4
   Tourists pick up, SH 7:4
   Breaking wind, SH 7:2

Kris Lindbeck
   Crochet mags, Twitter. <http://Twitter.com/KrisLindbeck>

Kozue Uzawa
   my acupuncturist, GUST 10

Larry Kimmel
   we did what we could, *Blue Night.*
   at first light, MET 12
   this time, she tells me, *Blue Night.*
   In Living Muscle, MHTP 2

Laurence Stacey
   home, *Haiku News.*

Lenard D. Moore
   on the number 4 train, RIBN 5:4

LeRoy Gorman
   how lived in, PRES 39
   the drone, GUST 9

Liam Wilkinson
   It comes down to this, Twitter. <http://twitter.com ldwilkinson>
   under the pier, *Darkening Tide.*
   bald, *Daily Haiga.*

Linda Galloway
   my daughter, [Third Place] *6th Intl Tanka Festival.*
   my name, RIBN 5:3
   every night, GUST 10

Linda Jeannette Ward
   softly, KOKA 11
   bikini-clad, BLTR 20
   clearing out, EUCL 6
   last fall's leaves, KOKA 10
   Downsized, MHTP 2

Lois Harvey
   that summer, GUST 9
Lorelei Jolie Polden
   the pointy chin, RIBN 5:2
M. Kei
   I don't want, *Heron Sea*.
   Melville, [Honorable Mention] *Saigyo Awards*.
   Sabbath morning, [Honorable Mention] [SFIT]
   cargo shorts, Twitter. <http://twitter.com/kujakupoet>
   she faded away, my mother, RIBN 5:3
   one son dead, *While the Light Holds*.
   they name, STLT
   my son does, WLOT 8
   Legs of Invisible Desire, ATPO 3
Magdalena Dale
   A dry leaf, ALBT 2009
Margaret Chula
   yesterday's desires, [First Place] *6th Intl Tanka Festival*.
   walking the path, [Members Choice] RIBN 5:2
M. L. Grace
   for thirty years, RIBN 5:3
   my wild side, EUCL 6
M. L. Harvey
   she never made, ATPO 3
   he searches, ATPO 4
Margarita Engle
   trapped, SGL
   feedstore, ATPO 3
Maria Steyn
   war zone, EUCL 6
Marilyn Hazelton
   I imagine myself, GUST 9
Marilyn Potter
   beside the sea, RIBN 5:4
Marian Morgan
   it should have been, EUCL 6
Mark Rutter
   too deep in the cave, PRES 39
Mary Mageau
   our family, GUST 10
Max Ryan
   work boots, EUCL 7
Megan Arkenberg
   late spring, MET 12
Melissa Dixon
   past midnight, REDL 5:2
   awakening, SGL

Michael Ketchek
  in the decanter, RIBN 5:3
Michael McClintock
  and one day, BTLR 20
  starting home, today, MET 11
  black-and-white. MET 12
  in a city, GUST 9
  I'm a recluse, GUST 9
  enough is enough, [Honorable Mention] [SFIT]
  I want to join, REDL 5:1
  at the bottom, STLT
  The Egyptian Exhibit, MHTP 1
Miriam Sagan
  At the wedding, *Tanka from the Edge.*
  in the dream, Ibid
  It wasn't snow, Ibid
  the flowers, Ibid
  farmer's market, Ibid
Natalia L. Rudychev
  somehow, REDL 5:2
Owen Bullock
  I know, MET 11
  quiet evening, PRES 38
  she leaves today, KOKA 11
Pamela A. Babusci,
  the knife slips so easily, *A Thousand Reasons.*
  breaking, Ibid
  don't ask, Ibid
  alone in spring, Ibid
  bringing a pot of coffee, Ibid
  a van Gogh, RIBN 5:1
  one-way ticket, REDL 5:2
Pamela Cooper
  last round of chemo, GUST 10
Pamela Miller Ness
  Autumn, REDL 5:1
Patricia Prime
  this is the park bench, [Honorable Mention] *Lyrical Passion for Poetry Tanka Contest.*
  without him, MET 12
  I watch, BLTH 19:2
Patrick M. Pilarski
  waking up, *Huge Blue.*
  the day, Ibid
Paul O. Williams
  my wife, REDL 5:2
  the old couple, REDL 5:1

Paul Smith
  after your death, *Paper Moon : Tanka and Other Short Form Poetry.*
  watching a moth, MET 11
  facing me, MET 11
Peggy Heinrich
  dropping, RIBN 5:2
Philip Miller,
  a shadow, EUCL 7
Philomene Kocher
  four years on this street, GUST 9
R. K. Singh
  At the river, *Selected Poems of R. K. Singh.*
Randy Brooks
  I sit on the edge, RIBN 5:3
Raquel D. Bailey
  rising from the earth, MET 12
Reiko Nakagawa, with William Elliott
  My hands are numb, TTJ 35
robert d. wilson
  sundown, *Jack Fruit Moon.*
  trash piled, Ibid
  may i, *Wonderland Amusement Park.*
  i wish i, Ibid
  buddha Ibid
  twilight, *Jack Fruit Moon.*
  a leather doll, Ibid
Robert Kusch
  singing, RIBN 5:4
Roberta Beary
  all those years, STLT
  I fight the urge, SGL
Roger Jones
  bang bang bang, MET 12
Ruth Holzer
  saffron and black, WIST 13
Sanford Goldstein
  like some modern, SGL
  after, PRUJ 2
  I look beyond, BTLR 20
  my corridor pace, *Rusty Tea Kettle 1.*
  I stroke, REDL 5:2
  I rise, GUST 9
  faces, GUST 10
  another, ATPO 4
Sean Greenlaw
  empty, Twitter. <http://Twitter.com/spgreenlaw>

twenty three dollars, Ibid
next to me, Twitter. Ibid
stanley pelter
she hides her tooth, ATPO 3
Susan Marie La Vallee
first star of the night, REDL 5:2
Terry Ann Carter
under a yellow parasol, GUST 9
nothing lives, *Yangtze Crossing.*
Thelma Mariano
winter's end, GUST 9
Tom Clausen
the house quiet, STLT
the farther away it gets, REDL 5:2
autumn chill, STLT
years of thinking, *Rusty Tea Kettle 1.*
in the park, STLT
all these years, *Tanka Online.*
Vasile Moldovan
After the flock's, *Haiku : Journal of the Romanian Haiku Society.* RO, 2009.
William Hart
the centre, BTLR 20

Venues Consulted, 2009

In order to be eligible for consideration, a work had to be a finished, available to the general public and published during 2009. All abbreviations from 'Tanka Venues,' as approved for use by the Tanka Society of America, <http://TankaCentral.com>.

Print Periodicals
Albatros: The Journal of the Constanta Haiku Society. [ALBT] Constanta, Romania, 2009.
Atlas Poetica : A Journal of Poetry of Place in Modern English Tanka. Kei, M., ed. [ATPO] Baltimore, MD: MET Press, 2009.
Blithe Spirit Journal : Journal of the British Haiku Society. [BLTH] London, UK: British Haiku Society, 2009.
bottle rockets. Stanford Forrester, ed. [BTLR] Windsor, CT: bottle rockets Press, 2009.
Concise Delight. Baltimore, MD: MET Press, 2009. <http://www.concisedelight.com/>
Eucalypt : A Tanka Journal. [EUCL] Pearl Beach, AUS, 2009.
Gusts : Contemporary Tanka. [GUST] Burnaby, BC: Tanka Canada, 2009.
Haiku Canada Review. Napanee, ON, CAN: Haiku Canada, 2009.
Haiku : Journal of the Romanian Haiku Society. Bucharest, RO, 2009.
HPNC Newsletter #49. San Francisco, CA: Haiku Poets of Northern California, 2009.
Hummingbird : Magazine of the Short Poem. [HBRD] Richland Center, WI, 2009.
Kokako. [KOKA] Te Atatu South, Auckland, NZ, 2009.
Lilliput Review. [LILR] Pittsburg, PA: Lilliput Review, 2009.
Magnapoets : taking over the world one poem at a time. [MAGP] Tecumseh, ONT, 2009.
Mariposa. [MARI] San Francisco, CA: Haiku Poets of Northern California, 2009.
Modern English Tanka. [MET] Baltimore, MD: MET Press, 2009.
Modern Haibun and Tanka Prose. Baltimore, MD: Modern English Tanka Press, 2009. ISSN 1947-606X
Modern Haiga : Presenting Modern Graphic Poetry at Its Best. [MDHG] Baltimore, MD: MET Press, 2009. ISSN 1941-4986 <http://www.ModernHaiga.com>
moonset / literary newspaper /. [MNST] La Pine, OR: the natal * light press, 2009.
Noon : Journal of the Short Poem. [NOON] Tokyo, JP, 2009.
Paper Wasp. [PAPW] Chapel Hill, Queensland, AUS, 2009.
Presence. [PRES] Preston, UK, 2009.

Prune Juice : A Journal of Senyru and Kyoka. [PRUJ] Baltimore, MD: MET Press, 2009.
red lights : a tanka journal. [REDL] New York, NY, 2009.
Ribbons : Tanka Society of America Journal. [RIBN] Baltimore, MD: MET Press, 2009.
The Taj Mahal Review : An International Journal Devoted To Arts, Literature, Poetry And Culture. India. 2009. ISSN 0972-6004
The Tanka Journal. [TTJ] Tokyo, JP: Nihon Kaijin (Tanka Poet Club), 2009.
Time Haiku. London, UK: Time Haiku Group, 2009.
White Lotus Journal. [WLOT] Excelsior Springs, MO: Shadow Poetry, 2009.
Wisteria : A Journal of Haiku, Senryu, & Tanka. [WIST] Lufkin, TX, 2006–

Anthologies & Contests
Antonovic, Aurora, et al. eds. *One Hundred Droplets : Magnapoets Anthology Series 1.* Tecumseh, ONT, Magnaprints, 2009.
Antonovic, Aurora, et al. eds. *While the Light Holds : Magnapoets Anthology Series 2.* Tecumseh, ON, CAN: Magnaprints, 2009.
Bruce, Dawn & Greg Piko, eds. *Wind Over Water : an anthology of haiku and tanka.* Pearl Beach, AUS: Beverley George, 2009.
Friendly Street Tanka and Tanka Sequence Contest. 2009. <http://ootawriters.blogspot.com/2009/04/friendly-street-poets-inc-japanese.html>
Garrison, Denis M. *Haiku Harvest : 2000– 2006.* San Francisco, CA: Scribd.com, 2009. [e-book]
George, Beverley, ed. *First Words : A Eucalypt Challenge.* Pearl Beach, AUS: Eucalypt, 2009. No ISBN [email anthology]
George, Beverley, ed. *Year of the Cow/Ox : A Eucalypt Challenge.* Pearl Beach, AUS: Eucalypt, 2009. No ISBN [email anthology]
Haiku Poets of Northern California. *San Francisco International Competition : Tanka Contest.* [SFIT] San Francisco, CA: HPNC, 2009.
Japan Tanka Poets' Society. *6th Intl Tanka Festival.* Tokyo, JP, 2009.
Kokako Tanka Contest. Te Atatu South, Auckland, NZ: Kokako, 2009.
Kolodji, Deborah, P. & Stephen M. Wilson, eds. *Dwarf Stars* 2009. Covina, CA: Science Fiction Poetry Society, 2009.
Lyrical Passion for Poetry Tanka Contest. 2009. <http://lyricalpassionpoetry.yolasite.com/2009-world-tanka-contest.php>
Mankh, ed. *Haiku and Brush Calligraphy Calendar 2009.* Seldon, NY: Allbooks, 2009.
McClintock, Michael and Denis M. Garrison, eds. *Streetlights : Urban Poetry in Modern English Tanka.* [STLT] Baltimore, MD: MET Press, 2009. ISBN 978-1-935398-04-2

Best Contemporary Tanka

McClintock, Michael and Karen McClintock, eds. *Poetry and Art Postcards (Series Three)*. Fresno, CA: Three Fountains Press, 2009. No ISBN.
Reichhold, Jane, ed. *Tanka Splendor Awards*. [TSPL] Gualala, CA: AHA Books, 2009. <http://AHAPoetry.com>
Reichhold, Jane, ed. *Twenty Years of Tanka Splendor*. Gualala, CA: AHA Books, 2009. <http://AHAPoetry.com>
Siddiqui, Mohammed H., ed. *Season's Greeting Letter : Ocean-Sea*. [SGL] Baltimore, MD: Mohammed H. Siddiqui, 2009.
Tanka Society of America. *International Tanka Contest*. 2009.
Thomas, Carolyn, ed. *The Saigyo Awards for Tanka 2009*. Hemet, CA, 2009.

Works by Individual Authors
Babusci, Pamela A. *A Thousand Reasons : Tanka*. Rochester, NY: Pamela A. Babusci, 2009. No ISBN
Carter, Terry Ann. *Yangtze Crossing*. Carleton Place, ONT: Bondi Studios. 2009.
Conforti, Gerard J. *Shells in the Sand*. Gualala, CA: AHA Books, 2009. ISBN 978-0-944676-32-
Conneally, Paul. *After Fern Hill*. San Francisco, CA: Scribd.com, 2009. <http://www.Scribd.com>
Coutu Radmore, Claudia. *Blackbird's Throat*. Carleton Place, ONT: Bondi Studios. 2009.
Diep, Phuoc-Tan. *Lights out & other poems. Wake up! series. Vol. 1*. San Francisco, CA: Scribd.com, 2009. <http://www.Scribd.com>
George, Beverley. *Drawing God and Other Pastimes*. Warner Bay, N.S.W. : Picaro Press, 2009.
Goldstein, Sanford. *Niigata Ars Nova*. Niigata, JP: Daishi Hall, 2009. No ISBN
Jacobsen, Gerry. *Awakening Albion*. London, UK: Coherent Visions, 2009.
Kei, M. *Heart of a Sailor*. World Class Poetry, 2009. <http://www.worldclasspoetryblog.com/category/world-class-poetry/> No ISBN.
Kei, M., *Heron Sea, Short Poems of the Chesapeake Bay*. San Francisco, CA: Scribd.com, 2009. <http://www.Scribd.com> No ISBN.
Kimmel, Larry. *Blue Night & the inadequacy of long-stemmed roses*. Baltimore, MD: MET Press, 2009. ISBN 978-1-935398-02-8
Kituai, Kathy. *Straggling Into Winter*. Morrisville, NC: Lulu Enterprises, 2009. [e-book] ISBN 978-1-4587-1157-1
Kohut-Bartels, Jane. *A Seasoning of Lust*. Morrisville, NC: Lulu Enterprises, 2009. ISBN 978-0-578-01232-2

Lauber, Maurice. *A Love Affair with Poetry*. Morrisville, NC: Lulu Enterprises, 2009. ISBN 978-0-557-05815-0

Lebel, Gary D. *Abacus : Prose poems, haibun and short poems*. San Francisco, CA: Scribd.com, 2009. No ISBN [e-book]<http://www.Scribd.com>

LeBlanc, Jean. *The Stream Singing Your Name : Tanka and Sijo*. Baltmore, MD: MET Press, 2009. ISBN 978-1-935398-06-6

Morcom, Joanne. *about the blue moon*. Edmonton, AB: Inkling, Press, 2009.

Pelter, Stanley. *slightly scented short lived words and roses*. Easton, Winchester, Hampshire, UK: George Mann Publications, 2009. No ISBN

Pilarski, Patrick M. *Huge Blue*. Lantzville, BC: Leaf Press, 2009. ISBN 978-1-926655-02-4

Reichhold, Jane. *Scarlet Scissors Fire*. Gualala, CA: AHA Books, 2009. <http://AHAPoetry.com> ISBN 978-0-944676-46-2

Reichhold, Jane, and Werner Reichhold. *A Film of Words*. Gualala, CA: AHA Poetry, 2009. ISBN 978-0-557-13424-3

Rogers, Kate. *Shape of Things to Come*. San Francisco, CA: Scribd.com, 2009. <http://www.Scribd.com>

Rotella, Alexis. *Elvis in Black Leather, A Tanka Poetry Collection*. Baltimore, MD: Modern English Tanka Press, 2009. ISBN 978-1-935398-09-7

Rotella, Alexis. *Lip Prints : Tanka Collection 1979– 2007*. San Francisco, CA: Scribd.com, 2009. No ISBN. [e-book] <http://www.Scribd.com>

Rotella, Alexis. *Looking for a Prince : A Collection of Senryu and Kyoka*. San Francisco, CA: Scribd.com, 2009. No ISBN [e-book] <http://www.Scribd.com>

Sagan, Miriam. *Tanka from the Edge*. Baltimore, MD: MET Press, 2009.

Singh, R. K. *Selected Poems of R. K. Singh : 1974– 2009*. Morrisville, NC: Lulu Enterprises, 2009.

Snow, Steaven R. *Buffet of the Mind*. Frederick, MD: PublishAmerica, 2009. ISBN 978-1608131488

Swanson, Amy Meredith. *Soul Expressions . . . Poetry for Thought by Amy Merideth Swanson*. San Francisco, CA: Scribd.com, 2009. <Scribd.com>

Tipton, James. *All the Horses of Heaven / Todos los Caballos del Paraíso*. Martha Alcántar, trans. Baltimore, MD: MET Press, 2009. ISBN 978-1-935398-05-9

Verbeke, Geert. *IJS / ICE*. Kortrijk, Belgium: Geert Verbeke, 2009. No ISBN

Ward, Linda Jeannette. *A Delicate Dance of Wings*. Morrisville, NC: Clinging Vine & Winifred Press, 2009.

Wilkinson, Liam. *Darkening Tide*. San Francisco, CA: Scribd.com, 2009. <http://www.Scribd.com>

Wilson, Robert. *Jack Fruit Moon : Haiku and Tanka.* Baltimore, MD: MET Press, 2009. ISBN 978-0-9817691-4-1

Yuhki, Aya, and Anna Holley. *Spreading Ripples.* Tokyo, JP: Banraisha Publishing Company, 2009.

Websites and Online Journals
3Lights Gallery. 2009. <http://threelightsgallery.com>
Bolts of Silk : beautiful poetry with something to say. 2009. <http://boltsofsilk.blogspot.com>
Chrysanthemum. 2009. <http://members.aon.at/bregen/>
Contemporary Haibun Online : A Quarterly Journal of Contemporary English Language Haibun. 2009. <http://contemporaryhaibunonline.com>
Daily Haiga : An Edited Journal of Contemporary & Traditional Haiga. 2009. <http://www.dailyhaiga.org>
Dragonfly Archives. (formerly the Dragonfly Collection). 2009. <http://dragonflyarchives.wordpress.com/>
GS Poetry— The Ultimate Poetry and Writing Community. 2009. <http://www.gspoetry.com/poemlisting.php>
Haibun Today : The State of the Art. 2009. <http://haibuntoday.blogspot.com>
Haiga of the Month. 2009. <http://haiku-wortart-forum.de/Forum24-1.aspx>
HaigaOnline : A Journal of Poetry and Painting. 2009. <http://www.haigaonline.com>
Haiku du Jour. 2009. <mankh9@pafcu.net>
Haiku News. 2009. <http://www.wayfarergallery.net/haikunews>
Ink, Sweats, and Tears : the poetry & prose webzine: Haibun, Haiku & Haiga. 2009. <http://ink-sweat-and-tears.blogharbor.com/blog/>
Just Tanka. 2009. <http://community.livejournal.com/just_tanka/>
Loch Raven Review. 2009. <http://www.lochravenreview.net/>
Lynx : a journal for linking poets. [LYNX] Gualala, CA: AHA Poetry, 2009. <http://AHAPoetry.com>
Muse India the Literary Journal. 2009. <http://www.museindia.com>
New Verse News. 2009. <http://www.newversenews.com>
Notes From the Gean : A Journal of Japanese Short Forms. 2009- <http://geantree.com/index.html>
Rusty Tea Kettle. 2009. <http://rustyteakettle.blogspot.com>
Scifaikuest. 2009. <http://www.samsdotpublishing.com/scifaikuest/contents.htm>
Simply Haiku : A Quarterly Journal of Japanese Short Form Poetry. <http://www.simplyhaiku.com/>
Sketchbook : A Journal for Eastern and Western Short Forms. <http://poetrywriting.org/Sketchbook0-0Home/>

Stylus Poetry Journal. [STYL] AUS, 2009. <http://www.styluspoetryjournal.com>
Tanka Corner. 2009- <http://lyricalpassionpoetry.yolasite.com/modern-tanka-corner.php>
TankaNetz. 2009. <TankaNetz.de>
Tanka Online. 2009. <http://tankaonline.com/>
Tobacco Road. 2010. <http://tobaccoroadpoet.com>
Twitter. 2009. <http://Twitter.com>
Twitwall. 2009. <http:twitwall.com>

Blogs, Personal Pages, Miscellaneous Online Works
Antolin, Susan. *Artichoke Season.* 2009. <http://artichokeseason.wordpress.com/>
Aoyagi, Fay. *Blue Willow World.* 2009. <http://fayaoyagi.wordpress.com/category/tanka/>
Arkenberg, Megan. *White Cherryblossoms.* 2009. <http://whitecherryblossoms.blogspot.com>
Barber, Collin. *Haiku, Tanka, Haiga & Haibun.* 2009. <http://collinbarber.com/45.html>
Bonfire Field : Just another WordPress.com weblog. 2009. <http://bonfirefield.wordpress.com/>
Cantey, Jack. *Jack Cantey's Home Page.* 2009. <http://jackcantey.wordpress.com/tag/urban-tanka>
Cook-Jolicoeur, Andrew. *My Very Gay Wedding.* 2009. <http://myverygaywedding.wordpress.com>
Dunlap, Curtis. *Tobacco Road Blog.* 2009. <http://tobaccoroadpoet.blogspot.com>
Kei, M. *Kujaku Poetry.* 2009. <http://kujakupoet.blogspot.com>
Kitakubo, Mariko. *Tanka Poet Mariko Kitakubo.* 2009. <http://tanka.kitakubo.com/english/>
Kolodji, Deborah P. *Poetry Scrapbook and Random Musings.* 2009. <http://dkolodji.livejournal.com/241869.html>
Leuck, Angela. *A Poet in the Garden.* 2009. <http://www.acleuck.blogspot.com>
Lilliput Review Blog. 2009. <http://LilliputReview.blogspot.com>
Liu, Chen-ou. *Stay Drunk on writing.* 2009. <http://ericcoliu.blogspot.com>
Lockhart, J. Andrew. *Past Tense : A Collection of Haiku, Tanka, Haiga, and Other Forms of Poetry.* 2009. <http://jamesalockhart.blogspot.com>
Magnapoets Japanese Form: Tanka. 2009. <http://www.magnapoets.com/magnapoets_japanese_form/tanka>
Murtha. H. Gene. *Miller's Pond : The Poetry of H. Gene Murtha.* 2009. <http://hgenemurtha.blogspot.com/2009/07/tanka-2008.html>

Roswila. *Dream and Poetry Realm.* 2009. <http://roswila-dreamspoetry.blogspot.com>
Rotella, Alexis. *Alexis Rotellas' Blog.* 2009. <http://alexisrotella.wordpress.com>
Rotella, Alexis. *Rotellagrams.* 2009. <http://alexisrotellapoetry.blogharbor.com>
Smith, Paul. *Paper Moon.* 2009. <http://tanka-papermoon.blogspot.com>
Stacey. *If You Want Kin, You Must Plant Kin.* 2009. <http://girlgriot.wordpress.com>
Sunny. *Time for Tanka : Capturing moments in 31 syllables.* 2009. <http://timefortanka.wordpress.com>
Turner, Martin. *Tankas for the Memory.* 2009. <http://mvlturner.wordpress.com/2009/05/04/tankas-for-the-memory>
Turner, Susan. *Tumblewords Blog.* 2009. <http://firsttumblewords.blogspot.com>
Von Vaupel, Alex. *Alex Von Vaupel dot com.* 2009. <http://alexvonvaupel.com>
Wilson, Robert. D. *Wonderland Amusement Park.* 2009. <http://thewonderlandamusementpark.blogspot.com>

EDUCATIONAL USE NOTICE

MODERN ENGLISH TANKA PRESS, Baltimore, Maryland, USA, publisher of the annual, *Take Five: Best Contemporary Tanka*, is dedicated to poetry education in schools and colleges, at every level. It is our intention and our policy to facilitate the use of *Take Five: Best Contemporary Tanka* and related materials to the maximum extent feasible by educators at every level of school and university studies. Educators, without individually seeking permission from the publisher, may make use of *Take Five: Best Contemporary Tanka* publications, online digital editions and print editions, as primary or ancillary teaching resources. Copyright law "Fair Use" guidelines and doctrine should be interpreted very liberally with respect to *Take Five: Best Contemporary Tanka* precisely on the basis of our explicitly stated intention herein. This statement may be cited as an effective permission to use *Take Five: Best Contemporary Tanka* as a text or resource for studies. Proper attribution of any excerpt to *Take Five: Best Contemporary Tanka* is required. This statement applies equally to digital resources and print copies of the journal. Individual copyrights of poets, authors, artists, etc., published in *Take Five: Best Contemporary Tanka* are their own property and are not meant to be compromised in any way by the journal's liberal policy on "Fair Use." Any educator seeking clarification of our policy for a particular use may email M. Kei, the Editor-in-chief of *Take Five: Best Contemporary Tanka*, at take5tanka@gmail.com. We welcome innovative uses of our resources for poetry education.

Index

A. A. Marcoff, 27
A. Thiagarajan, 27
Adelaide B. Shaw, 23, 157
ai li, 20, 28
Alex von Vaupel, 29
Alexis Rotella, 30-31, 172
Amelia Fielden, 32-33
An Xiao, 34
an'ya, 35
Ana-Maria DiVera, 34
André Surridge, 36
Andrew Cook-Jolicoeur, 37
Andrew Riutta, 38
Angela Leuck, 24, 39, 166-167
Annette Mineo, 40
Audrey Olberg, 41
Aurora Antonovic, 42
Aya Yuhki, 43
Barbara Strang, 43
Becky DeVito, 44
Belinda Broughton, 45
Bell Gale Chevigny, 45
Beverley George, 19, 46-47
Bob Lucky, 48-49, 158-159
C. W. Hawes, 50
C. William Hinderliter, 50
Carol Raisfeld, 51
Carole MacRury, 52
Carolyn Eldridge-Alfonzetti, 53
Carolyn Thomas, 54
Cathy Drinkwater Better, 55
Chad Lee Robinson, 56
Chen-ou Liu, 57
Cherie Hunter Day, 57
Claudia Coutu-Radmore, 58
Colin Stewart Jones, 58
Collin Barber, 59
Cor van den Heuvel, 60
Curtis Dunlap, 61
Cynthia Rowe, 62
Dave Bacharach, 63
Dave Bachelor, 64
David Lee Kirkland, 65

David Rice, 66
David Terelinck, 67
Dawn Bruce, 69
Deborah P. Kolodji, 68
Denis M. Garrison, 69
Don Miller, 70
Dorothy McLaughlin, 71
Elaine Riddell, 72
Ferris Gilli, 73
Francis Masat, 73
Gautam Nadkarni, 74
Geert Verbeke, 74
George Swede, 75
H. Gene Murtha, 76
J. Andrew Lockhart, 77
Jade Pandora, 78
James Tipton, 18, 79
Jane Reichhold, 80
Janet Lynn Davis, 81
Jared Carter, 170-171
Jean LeBlanc, 82
Jeanne Emrich, 83
Jeffrey Woodward, 84
Jo McInerney, 85
Joanne Morcom, 85
John Martell, 86
John Quinnett, 87
Joyce Sandeen Johnson, 87
June Moreau, 88
Kala Ramesh, 23, 89
Karen Cesar, 90
Kathy Kituai, 91
Kathy Lippard Cobb, 92
Kirsty Karkow, 93
Kisaburo Konoshima, 16-17, 94
Kozue Uzawa, 95
Kris Lindbeck, 96
Larry Kimmel, 23, 97, 160
Laurence Stacey, 98
Lenard D. Moore, 98
LeRoy Gorman, 99
Liam Wilkinson, 100
Linda Galloway, 101

Linda Jeannette Ward, 102, 161
Lois Harvey, 103
Lorelei Jolie Polden, 103
M. Kei, 104-105, 168
M. L. Grace, 106
M. L. Harvey, 107
Magdalena Dale, 108
Margaret Chula, 109
Margarita Engle, 110
Maria Steyn, 111
Marian Morgan, 113
Marilyn Hazelton, 112
Marilyn Potter, 112
Mark Rutter, 114
Mary Mageau, 114
Max Ryan, 115
Megan Arkenberg, 115
Melissa Dixon, 116
Michael Ketchek, 117
Michael McClintock, 118-119, 162
Miriam Sagan, 120-121
Natalia L. Rudychev, 122
Owen Bullock, 123
Pamela A. Babusci, 124-125
Pamela Cooper, 126
Pamela Miller Ness, 127
Patricia Prime, 128
Patrick M. Pilarski, 129
Paul O. Williams, 130
Paul Smith, 131
Peggy Heinrich, 132
Philip Miller, 132
Philomene Kocher, 133
R. K. Singh, 134
Randy Brooks, 134
Raquel D. Bailey, 135
Reiko Nakagawa, 138
robert d. wilson, 136-137
Robert Kusch, 20, 139
Roberta Beary, 140
Roger Jones, 141
Ruth Holzer, 141
Sanford Goldstein, 18, 21, 142-143
Sean Greenlaw, 17, 144
stanley pelter, 145

Susan Marie La Vallee, 146
Terry Ann Carter, 147
Tess Driver, 148
Thelma Mariano, 149
Tom Clausen, 150-151
Vasile Moldovan, 152
William Hart, 153
William I. Elliott, 138

Also from MODERN ENGLISH TANKA PRESS

Home toBallygunge: Kolkata Tanka ~ William Hart

Black Jack Judy and the Crisco Kids: Bronx Memories ~ Tanka by Alexis Rotella

Where We Go: haiku and tanka sequences and other concise imaginings by Jean LeBlanc.

The Time of This World: 100 tanka from 13 collections by Kawano Yuko, trans. Amelia Fielden & Saeko Ogi.

Peeling an Orange ~ Haiku by Peggy Heinrich. Photographs by John Bolivar.

A Breath of Surrender: A Collection of Recovery-Oriented Haiku ~ Robert Epstein, Ed.

A Poetic Guide to an Ancient Capital: Aizu Yaichi and the City of Nara ~ Michael F. Marra

Elvis In Black Leather ~ Tanka by Alexis Rotella

The Stream Singing Your Name ~ Tanka and Sijo by Jean LeBlanc

Streetlights: Poetry of Urban Life in Modern English Tanka ~ Michael McClintock & Denis M. Garrison, Eds..

Take Five: Best Contemporary Tanka ~ Anthology. M. Kei, Sanford Goldstein, Pamela A. Babusci, Patricia Prime, Bob Lucky & Kala Ramesh, Eds.

All the Horses of Heaven ~ Tanka by James Tipton

Blue Night & the inadequacy of long-stemmed roses / The Temperature of Love (2nd Ed.) ~ Larry Kimmel

Tanka from the Edge ~ Miriam Sagan

Jack Fruit Moon ~ Robert D. Wilson

Meals at Midnight ~ Poems by Michael McClintock

Lilacs After Winter ~ Francis Masat

Proposing to the Woman in the Rear View Mirror ~ Haiku & Senryu by James Tipton.

Abacus: Prose poems, haibun & short poems ~ Gary LeBel

Looking for a Prince: a collection of senryu and kyoka ~ Alexis Rotella

The Tanka Prose Anthology ~ Jeffrey Woodward, Ed.

Greetings from Luna Park ~ Sedoka, James R. Burns

In Two Minds ~ Responsive Tanka by Amelia Fielden and Kathy Kituai

An Unknown Road ~ Haiku by Adelaide B. Shaw

Slow Motion: The Log of a Chesapeake Bay Skipjack ~ M. Kei

Ash Moon Anthology: Poems on Aging in Mod. Engl. Tanka ~ Alexis Rotella & Denis M. Garrison, Eds.

Fire Blossoms: The Birth of Haiku Noir ~ haiku noirs by Denis M. Garrison

Cigarette Butts and Lilacs: tokens of a heritage ~ Tanka by Andrew Riutta

Sailor in the Rain and Other Poems ~ free and formal verse by Denis M. Garrison

Four Decades on My Tanka Road ~ Sanford Goldstein. Fran Witham, Ed.

this hunger, tissue-thin: new & selected tanka 1995–2005 ~ Larry Kimmel

Jun Fujita, Tanka Pioneer ~ Denis M. Garrison, Ed.

Landfall: Poetry of Place in Mod. English Tanka ~ Denis M. Garrison and Michael McClintock, Eds.

Lip Prints: Tanka . . . 1979-2007 ~ Alexis Rotella

Ouch: Senryu That Bite ~ Alexis Rotella

Eavesdropping: Seasonal Haiku ~ Alexis Rotella

Five Lines Down: A Landmark in English Tanka ~ Denis M. Garrison, Ed.

Tanka Teachers Guide ~ Denis M. Garrison, Ed.

Sixty Sunflowers: TSA Members' Anthology 2006-2007 ~ Sanford Goldstein, Ed.

The Dreaming Room: Mod. Engl. Tanka in Collage & Montage Sets ~ M. McClintock & D.M. Garrison, Eds.

The Salesman's Shoes ~ Tanka, James Roderick Burns

Hidden River ~ Haiku by Denis M. Garrison

The Five-Hole Flute: Mod. Engl. Tanka in Sequences & Sets ~ D.M. Garrison & M. McClintock, Eds.